Endorsements

"America is in desperate need of revival. I pray to the One who is able to do immeasurably more than all we ask or imagine that we see revival in our homes, communities, and our nation. Congratulations, Chris Widener, on the book, and thank you for your prayer for revival again here in America."

~Senator Tim Scott

"Chris Widener has written a groundbreaking book that contains a chronology of how our churches and nation have eroded and what we must do to remedy it. *The Coming American Revival* addresses the elephant in the room—and if not addressed, America falls. This insightful and straightforward book should be on every pastor's desk and every Christian's list of "must-read" books. I'm ordering several for our pastors and our college professors!"

~Dr. Wayne Cordeiro,
New Hope Church & College, Eugene, Oregon

"This message in this book is absolutely critical for real Christians to read. The problems in our country will be dealt with when the Church has an actual, tangible revival. A weak Church makes for a weak nation. I hope it happens soon; the clock is ticking."

~John Rich, Singer, Songwriter

"Chris Widener's *The Coming American Revival* poignantly addresses the deep spiritual crisis in America, calling for a return to godly principles as the true remedy for a nation in spiritual decline. It captures the cyclical nature of human faithfulness and rebellion, reminding us of the need for repentance, which precedes revival. The vision of a restored humanity rooted in Christ is both hopeful and challenging, urging believers to take action in their communities and spread the message of Jesus. As pastors, we must heed this call, boldly proclaim the truth, and lead our congregations in seeking God's face for the healing of all those we are called to love."

**~Jason Fritz, Lead Pastor,
Illuminate Community Church, Scottsdale, AZ**

"*The Coming American Revival* is a clarion call to the Church that it's time to get serious about the pursuit of God. The stakes are high for our country, and revival is the only answer!"

~Kevin Sorbo, Actor, Director, Author

"This is a timely book for our country! We need a revival, and Chris powerfully shares how we can experience it individually and together."

**~Jon Gordon, 17-time bestselling
Author of *The One Truth* and *The Carpenter***

"Every Christian who cares about renewing faith in America should read *The Coming American Revival*. It is a powerful reminder that politics is important, but we must find our hope in God and turn our hearts back to Him. This book shows us how we can see a revival in this great nation."

**~Rebecca Weber, CEO of the Association of
Mature American Citizens (AMAC)**

"Chris Widener understands the risks and rewards of revival. America will either be reduced to an ideological ash heap swept into the corner of history or experience a vibrant renewal and resurrection of life-giving principles that inspire the world to follow in her footsteps. I wish every Christian would read and follow the instructions of this book!"

~Kirk Cameron, Actor, Filmmaker

"From beginning to end, Chris Widener accurately describes the spiritual precipice upon which America finds itself and the path to revival that, if followed by Christians and church leaders, will help save it from itself. The Coming American Revival is comprehensive, detailed, and rooted in scripture...a must-read and call to action for all Christians and for those who desire America to retain its leadership position as 'the city on a hill.'"

~Vice Admiral Yancy B. Lindsey, USN Ret.

"The Ziglar family, starting with my dad, Zig, has always loved God and loved America. America is in a tough place right now, but God isn't through with us yet. *The Coming American Revival* is the perfect book to show us how to bring America back into Biblical values by seeking God's face and asking Him to revive us!"

~Tom Ziglar, President, Ziglar Companies

"Since 2020, I have been witnessing a revival. It isn't like the revivals of old. It is grassroots, underground. It is the Holy Spirit incarnate. Chris Widener's book, *The Coming American Revival*, will accelerate and perpetuate this historical event. If you want to see and understand revival, buy this book."

~Rev. Dr. Robert A. Schuller

"Wake up, everyone! *The Coming American Revival* won't happen without us. America was founded on God's Word, but we are giving God a million reasons not to love or care for us, yet He does. Chris Widener shares the recipe for Revival, and it's time for the chefs to enter the kitchen. Take a stand; your courage will strengthen the spine of others."

~Donna Johnson,
Author of *My Mentor Walks on Water*

"We must do all that we can to help America thrive, but I also know that ultimately, America's success depends on the blessing of God's hand upon our nation. Chris Widener's book, *The Coming American Revival*, challenges us to again turn toward God and seek His revival."

~Congressman Chuck Fleischmann

"The newest release from author Chris Widener, *The Coming American Revival*, is a combination wake-up call and map to sanity that our country so desperately needs. Read it now and be amazed at the trail about to be blazed."

~Andy Andrews, *NYT* Bestselling Author of
The Traveler's Gift* and *The Noticer

"*The Coming American Revival* is a great challenge to all of us to turn toward God and seek His revival, not only for ourselves but our churches and our nation. We live in challenging times, but this book will inspire you to know that God is in control, and He wants to bring revival to America."

~Todd Stottlemyre,
Two-Time World Series Winning Pitcher

"Alarmed by the moral and spiritual condition of America? While politics is important, it's downstream of the Church and isn't the ultimate solution. After all, Israel had the very laws of God, but they were still judged because their hearts were far from God! We need a spiritual revival to save America, and Chris Widener brilliantly shows what you can do to make Jesus the center of your life and help ignite a revival. Be the change you want to see - read and heed the biblical wisdom found here!"

~Frank Turek, CrossExamined.org, Co-Author of
I Don't Have Enough Faith to be an Atheist

"For survival, we want a God-centered revival! Chris Widener is leading the pack with how it WILL happen. We can go into the most extraordinary time ever. Enjoy reading this power-packed book."

~Mark Victor Hansen,
Co-author of the *Chicken Soup for the Soul* series,
***ASK!*, and the *One Minute Millionaire* series**

"In Chris Widener's new book, *The Coming American Revival*, you will not only learn about the historical significance of revival in America but you will also be provided with a strategy to spread revival in all areas of our nation. Chris lays out a 31-day devotional that will arm you with action steps to help spread revival in America."

~Herbert I. Burns, Jr, Award-winning Christian Author, Artist,
Architect, and Co-host of "Three Men for Thee"

THE COMING AMERICAN REVIVAL

THE BIBLICAL BLUEPRINT FOR IGNITING A NATION'S SOUL

Chris Widener

MADE FOR GRACE

Made for Success Publishing

www.MadeforSuccess.com

Distributed by Made for Success Publishing
Library of Congress Cataloging-in-Publication data

Widener, Chris
    The Coming American Revival: The Biblical Blueprint for Igniting a Nation's Soul

ISBN: 978-1-64146-912-8 (Paperback)
ISBN: 978-1-64146-913-5 (eBook)
ISBN: 978-1-64146-914-2 (Audiobook)

To Denise, my beautiful bride and partner
in seeking revival.

And to the faithful men and women who are diligent in prayer,
seeking God's face, asking for Him to bring revival to America again!

CONTENTS

revival /rĭ-vī'vəl/

Restoration to life, consciousness, vigor, strength.

To come to life again.

America sits in a precarious place. The once mighty "greatest country in the world" is broken and fractured. Division is rampant, driven by nefarious forces of evil, seeking to destroy a country that once stood as a "city on the hill," brightly lighting up the world with the hope of Jesus, freedom, and justice.

Now we see that the vast majority of people in America have turned away from God. Even those who say that they are Christians live as though they are not. Unholiness abounds. Sick sexuality is proclaimed from the rooftops through music, television, and entertainment. Violence overflows through our cities. Our streets are overrun with crime and poverty.

We drift because of a lack of godly leadership. Most of our politicians are unethical at best and criminals at worst. Our pastors will not proclaim the Word of God for fear that they will offend someone. Our teachers are more interested in grooming children's aberrant sexualities than teaching them to read and write. Too many children are raised in single-parent homes, stripping them of the chance to grow up with the leadership of a mother and father. We are indeed sheep without a shepherd.

Yes, America once lived for God, proclaimed Him through the world, sent missionaries across the globe, and donated billions of dollars of our wealth to help the unfortunate, far and wide. We were admired.

Countries knew that we were a nation of Christians intent on proclaiming His glory.

But something happened. It is, in essence, the same thing that has happened for thousands of years. God's people have gone through the same cycle for millennia:

1. They love God and serve Him.
2. He blesses them with many blessings.
3. They get fat and happy and turn from God and instead, they worship their wealth and blessings.
4. God strips them of their blessings to draw them back to Himself.
5. The people fight and rebel and wallow in their sins.
6. Tired, they finally repent and realize they have turned their backs on God.
7. God, seeing their heartfelt repentance, brings them new life through revival.
8. They love God and serve Him

... And it continues.

So where are we now in this cycle? I believe we are moving firmly into number six. We are definitely fighting and rebelling and wallowing in our sins. But there is a cry that is beginning to be heard. It is the cry of those who have a vision of what could be. It is the cry that recognizes our complete and total dependence on God and sees how we have turned away from Him to worship false Gods. It is the cry of those who long for restoration. It is the cry of people who want God to be glorified and lifted up in our nation once more. I believe it is a cry that God Himself hears...

One of two things will happen now. One result is that we will continue in our wicked ways and our nation will eventually fall. Many do not believe that a mighty nation like America could ever fall. Those who believe that have forgotten the history of the Roman, Ottoman, and Mongolian Empires, all once mighty, world-controlling empires.

Nations rise and nations fall. The second outcome is revival. This would come only if the remnants of God's Church cry out, find critical mass, and bring our prayers before the throne of grace, asking God to forgive us of our sins and restore our nation.

At this point, I don't know what will happen. I do believe that God is raising up people who recognize our need as a nation and are calling for the people to repent and redirect themselves toward God. Some will heed the call, and some won't. I believe that if enough people turn their hearts to God, He will hear our prayers and will again make America the great nation it once was.

America, a nation once founded on biblical principles, now finds itself at a crossroads. In the past, the United States was seen as a "city upon a hill," a beacon of hope and morality rooted in Christian values. Today, however, many argue that America is under God's judgment due to its departure from those foundational principles. This chapter seeks to explore the reasons behind this perceived judgment and to offer a biblical pathway to revival through the actions of the church.

The Biblical Basis for God's Judgment

The Bible is replete with examples of nations and peoples falling under God's judgment due to their disobedience and sin. One of the clearest examples is found in the history of Israel, God's chosen people, who faced severe consequences when they turned away from His commandments. In Deuteronomy 28, God outlines blessings for obedience and curses for disobedience. Deuteronomy 28:15 warns, "But it shall come about, if you do not obey the Lord your God, to be careful to follow all His commandments and His statutes which I am commanding you today, that all these curses will come upon you and overtake you."

Similarly, Proverbs 14:34 states, "Righteousness exalts a nation, but sin is a disgrace to any people." America's current state can be viewed through this lens, as it appears to have strayed from righteousness and embraced sin in various forms.

Moral and Spiritual Decline

One of the primary reasons for God's judgment of America is the nation's moral and spiritual decline. The rise of secularism, moral relativism, and the rejection of absolute truth have led to a society where anything goes. The biblical worldview, which once undergirded American culture, has been replaced by a worldview that denies God and exalts humanism.

The legalization and normalization of behaviors that the Bible condemns as sins, such as abortion, same-sex marriage, and various forms of sexual immorality, are stark indicators of this decline. In Romans 1:18-32, the Apostle Paul describes the consequences of such behaviors, stating that God's wrath is revealed against all ungodliness and unrighteousness of men who suppress the truth in sin. He goes on to explain that because they did not acknowledge God, God gave them over to a debased mind, to do things which are not fitting.

Rejection of God and His Word

Another significant reason for America's judgment is the widespread rejection of God and His Word. The Bible, once revered and respected, is now often dismissed or ridiculed. Many people no longer see it as the ultimate authority on matters of faith and practice. This rejection is not limited to the secular world but has infiltrated the church as well. Many churches have compromised biblical truth in favor of cultural relevance, leading to a diluted and powerless gospel. We even have pastors who teach that the Bible is not relevant today.

In Hosea 4:6, God laments, "My people are destroyed for lack of knowledge. Since you have rejected knowledge, I also will reject you from being My priest. Since you have forgotten the Law of your God,

I also will forget your children." This verse highlights the danger of rejecting God's Word and the inevitable consequences that follow.

Social Injustice and Corruption

Social injustice and corruption are also indicators of a nation under judgment. The Bible repeatedly calls for justice and righteousness in the treatment of others. Micah 6:8 reminds us, "He has told you, mortal one, what is good; and what does the Lord require of you but to do justice, to love kindness, and to walk humbly with your God?"

Yet America is plagued with social injustices, including racial discrimination, economic inequality, and a lack of care for the vulnerable and marginalized. These injustices are a sign that the nation has strayed from God's commands and is suffering the consequences.

I know that many in the evangelical community have rejected anything that talks about "social justice" because of how that term has been perverted by apostate churches who turn the whole gospel into works-based social justice, but we must realize that God still calls us to be peacemakers and to stand for and defend the poor and destitute, the widows and orphans, and those who cannot help themselves. We cannot throw out the baby with the bathwater. There are some who preach Marxism wrapped in a veneer of Christian language and that is certainly to be rejected, but Christ's words to love "the least of these" cannot.

The Role of the Church in Revival

Despite the grim picture, there is hope. The church holds the key to revival and the potential to thwart God's judgment. Revival begins with the people of God recognizing their own need for repentance and turning back to Him with sincere hearts. 2 Chronicles 7:14 offers a timeless prescription for revival: "My people who are called by My name humble themselves, and pray and seek My face, and turn from their wicked ways, then I will hear from Heaven, and I will forgive their sin and will heal their land." You see, God *wants to bring revival*, but it is dependent on His people positioning themselves for it. If we aren't right, if we do not thirst for God, He waits. He doesn't waste His glory on unwelcoming people.

Humility and Repentance

The first step towards revival is humility and repentance. The church must acknowledge its own shortcomings and sins. Pride, complacency, and compromise have crept into many congregations, diluting the gospel's power. Revivalist Charles Finney once said, "Revival is nothing else than a new beginning of obedience to God" (*Lectures on Revivals of Religion,* 1868).

The church must repent of its sins and return to a place of obedience, seeking God's face earnestly and turning away from wickedness. This involves personal and corporate repentance, acknowledging areas where we have fallen short, and committing to live in accordance with God's Word.

The word *repentance*, in both the Old and New Testaments, shows us that it doesn't come from just mental agreement with the concept, but acting on it. In the Old Testament, the Hebrew word for "repentance" is "שׁוּב" (shuv), which means "to turn back" or "return." This term conveys the idea of turning away from sin and returning to God, emphasizing a change in direction and a restored relationship with Him. In the New Testament, the Greek word for "repentance" is "μετάνοια» (metanoia), which means "a change of mind" or "a change of heart." This term goes beyond mere mental regret or emotional remorse; it signifies a profound transformation of one's mind and purpose, resulting in a *shift in behavior* and a commitment to follow God's will. Both terms highlight how repentance, when real, transforms people's behavior. It involves both an inward change of heart and an outward change of action.

Fervent Prayer

Prayer is the lifeline of revival. Throughout history, every great revival has been preceded by fervent, persistent prayer. The church must return to a place of fervent prayer, interceding for the nation and pleading with God for mercy and revival.

Acts 4:31 provides a powerful example of the early church's commitment to prayer: "And when they had prayed, the place where they had gathered together was shaken, and they were all filled with the Holy Spirit and began to speak the Word of God with boldness." When the church prays, God moves.

One of the most notable instances of a prayer movement sparking a great revival in America is the Fulton Street Revival of 1857-1858, also known as the Third Great Awakening. It began with a single man, Jeremiah Lanphier, a lay missionary in New York City. Concerned about the spiritual apathy and moral decline he observed, Lanphier started a weekly prayer meeting for businessmen at the Old Dutch North Church on Fulton Street. On September 23, 1857, he held the first meeting, but only six people attended. Despite the modest beginning, Lanphier persevered, and the meetings grew steadily.

As news of the prayer meetings spread, attendance surged, and the gatherings expanded to daily meetings in various locations throughout the city. The movement quickly caught fire, with similar prayer meetings springing up across the nation. People from all walks of life attended, seeking spiritual renewal and interceding for their communities and the nation. The Fulton Street Revival led to a widespread spiritual awakening, with an estimated one million people converting to Christianity. This revival not only revitalized the American Church but also had a profound impact on society, fostering a renewed commitment to social reform and missionary work.

I pray that God will raise up a group of people who will join me in praying for revival.

Bold Proclamation of the Gospel

The church must also boldly proclaim the gospel without compromise. In a culture that is increasingly hostile to biblical truth, it is essential that the church remains steadfast in preaching the full counsel of God. The Apostle Paul exhorted Timothy to "Preach the Word; be ready in season and out of season; correct, rebuke, and exhort, with great patience and instruction" (2 Timothy 4:2).

The gospel has the power to transform lives and societies. The church must not shy away from declaring the truth of God's Word, even when it is unpopular or countercultural. It is through the faithful preaching of the gospel that hearts are changed and revival is sparked.

Romans 10:17 says that faith comes by hearing the Word of God. Faith doesn't come by carefully crafted sermons, witty quotes and sayings, or motivational speeches wrapped up to look like sermons. No, faith comes when people hear the Word of God. Unfortunately, our pastors are not preaching the Word anymore in America. The message of the gospel is what saves. Romans 1:16 says, "For I am not ashamed of the gospel, for it is the power of God for salvation to everyone who believes." Our American pastors need to be bold in their preaching of the Word of God.

Loving Our Neighbors

Revival also involves a renewed commitment to loving our neighbors as ourselves. This means extending God's love and mercy to those in need. Jesus' parable of the Good Samaritan (Luke 10:30-37) serves as a powerful reminder of our responsibility to care for others, regardless of their background or circumstances.

The church must be a beacon of hope and compassion in a broken world, demonstrating the love of Christ through acts of kindness, justice, and mercy. As we live out the gospel in practical ways, we become a tangible expression of God's Kingdom on earth.

I John 3:17-18 says, "But whoever has worldly goods and sees his brother or sister in need, and closes his heart against him, how does the love of God remain in him? Little children, let's not love with word or with tongue, but in deed and truth."

Where Not to Place Your Hope

A nation's revival does not stem from the actions of political leaders or governmental policies but from a collective turning of hearts towards God. Throughout history, true and lasting change has always begun in the hearts of individuals who seek a renewed relationship with God through Jesus Christ. Political leaders can play a role in creating an environment conducive to moral and spiritual renewal, but they are not the source of revival. As Psalm 146:3-5 admonishes, "Do not trust in noblemen, in mortal man, in whom there is no salvation. His spirit departs, he returns to the earth; on that very day his plans perish. Blessed is he whose help is the God of Jacob, whose hope is in the Lord his God."

The power for genuine transformation comes from the Holy Spirit, who works in and through believers to bring about a change of heart and mind. Jesus promised His followers the gift of the Holy Spirit to guide, comfort, and empower them for the work of the Kingdom (John 14:16-17, Acts 1:8). It is through the Spirit that we can experience true revival, as He convicts the world of sin, righteousness, and judgment (John 16:8).

Moreover, placing our hope in political leaders can lead to disappointment and disillusionment. Leaders are fallible and often fail to meet our expectations. Jeremiah 17:5-7 warns, "This is what the Lord says: 'Cursed is the man who trusts in mankind and makes flesh his strength, and whose heart turns away from the Lord. for he will be like a bush in the desert, and will not see when prosperity comes, but will live in stony wastes in the wilderness, a land of salt that is not inhabited. Blessed is the man who trusts in the Lord, and whose trust is the Lord.'"

As Christians, our ultimate allegiance must be to Christ and His Kingdom. While we can and should engage in the political process and advocate for righteous policies, our faith and hope should remain firmly rooted in God. It is through a personal and communal relationship with Jesus, empowered by the Holy Spirit, that we can bring about the kind of spiritual renewal that transforms not just individuals, but entire nations.

In fact, the case could be made that historically places where political leaders are opposed to Christianity actually experience the fastest growing and deepest Christianity. There is an old saying that "the blood of the martyrs is the seed of the Church." When political leaders persecute Christians, you have to decide really quickly whether you are going to stay true to your faith or turn away.

The Path to Revival

America may be under God's judgment due to its moral and spiritual decline, rejection of God and His Word, and social injustices. However, the church holds the key to revival. By humbling ourselves, repenting, fervently praying, boldly proclaiming the gospel, and loving our neighbors, we can see a mighty move of God in our land.

As Jonathan Edwards, a key figure in the First Great Awakening, once said, "The task of every generation is to discover in which direction the Sovereign Redeemer is moving, then move in that direction." The church must seek to align itself with God's purposes and be an agent of change and revival in America.

Let us, as the Body of Christ, rise up with renewed fervor and commitment to see our nation turn back to God. The promise of 2 Chronicles 7:14 stands true: if we humble ourselves, pray, seek God's face, and turn from our wicked ways, He will hear from Heaven, forgive our sins, and heal our land. May we heed this call and be the catalyst for the coming American revival.

A Personal Relationship With God

Ultimately, revival is about bringing God's people into a vibrant personal relationship with God. God is a person to be known. He isn't simply something to learn about. When revival hits, we become intimately involved with the living God. There are a couple of passages from my favorite Christian book of all time, *The Pursuit of God* by A.W. Tozer (2008), that talk about this personal relationship that I want to share with you:

"God wills that we should push on into His Presence and live our whole life there. This is to be known to us in conscious experience. It is more than a doctrine to be held, it is a life to be enjoyed every moment of every day."

"The Bible is not an end in itself, but a means to bring men to an intimate and satisfying knowledge of God, that they may enter into Him, that they may delight in His Presence, may taste and know the inner sweetness of the very God Himself in the core and center of their hearts."

The end goal is a close, vibrant, and personal relationship with the living God!

I close with this quote from Revelation 3:20. While this was not spoken to us directly, I do believe that it demonstrates how God interacts with His people: "Behold, I stand at the door and knock; if anyone hears My voice and opens the door, I will come in to him and will dine with him, and he with Me."

God is here. He is knocking. He desires to revive us and have fellowship. Do you hear the knock? Can you hear His voice outside the door, calling you? He wants to come in. He wants fellowship with His Church.

Yet there is only one question: Will you open the door?

That is where it begins. I hope that this book shows you the need for revival, the beauty of it, the desire God has to bring it, and how our country can be saved if we only call on God.

Imagining Revival...

Imagine a society where every morning begins with families gathered together, reading the Bible and praying for guidance, wisdom, and strength to live according to God's will. As the sun rises, neighborhoods come alive with the sounds of worship music and the aroma of shared breakfasts. Neighbors regularly meet to encourage one another in their faith and discuss the Scriptures. Schools and workplaces start the day with prayer and a short devotional, setting a tone of humility, gratitude, and purpose for the day ahead.

Imagine a community where businesses operate with integrity and transparency, prioritizing ethical practices over profit. Employers and employees treat each other with respect and kindness, creating a workplace culture that reflects Christ's love. Decision-making processes are guided by biblical principles, and customer service goes beyond transactions, aiming to serve and bless others. Financial success is seen as an opportunity to give generously and invest in community projects, ensuring that no one goes without their basic needs met.

Imagine a government that seeks to uphold justice and righteousness, drawing from Biblical teachings to enact laws that protect the vulnerable and promote the common good. Leaders at every level are chosen for their godly character and wisdom, dedicating their service to God and the people they represent. Public policies are crafted with compassion and a commitment to fairness, addressing issues like poverty, healthcare, and education, with a heart for restoration and hope. National days of prayer and fasting bring the country together, uniting citizens in their desire for God's guidance and blessing.

Imagine churches overflowing with people eager to worship and learn more about God. Congregations are vibrant and active, with members participating in various ministries and outreach programs, sharing the gospel, and meeting the needs of their communities. Sunday services are a time of joyous celebration and deep reflection, and the love among believers is palpable. Discipleship and mentorship flourish, with seasoned Christians guiding new believers in their spiritual growth. Churches act as refuges and beacons of hope, drawing people from all walks of life into a transformative relationship with Jesus Christ.

Imagine a culture where the arts, media, and entertainment reflect biblical values and the beauty of God's Creation. Music, films, and literature inspire and uplift, conveying messages of truth, redemption, and love. Social media platforms are used to spread positivity, encouragement, and the gospel, fostering a virtual community of believers who support and pray for each other. Public discourse is marked by grace and respect, even in disagreements, as people strive to see and treat others as image-bearers of God.

Imagine individuals living with a profound sense of purpose and identity rooted in Christ. Personal relationships are characterized by selflessness, forgiveness, and a genuine desire to honor God in every interaction. Families are strong and united, with parents diligently teaching their children the ways of the Lord and setting an example of faith and obedience. People find joy and fulfillment in serving others, seeing their daily activities—whether mundane or extraordinary— as acts of worship. In this revival of biblical Christianity, life is lived abundantly to the glory of God, and the love of Christ transforms hearts, homes, and nations.

Imagine revival.

Preface
The Need for Revival

Revival has been a recurring theme throughout the history of Christianity, particularly within the context of American society. The term "revival" evokes images of passionate sermons, fervent prayer, and communities transformed by the power of the Holy Spirit. But beyond these images lies a profound truth: *Revival is an essential aspect of the Christian faith*, calling believers back to a vibrant, passionate, and transformative relationship with God. In this book, *The Coming American Revival*, we will explore the incredible need for a new revival in our time, drawing from historical precedents, examining the current state of American culture and spirituality, and outlining a vision for the future.

Historical Context of Revivals in America

To understand the need for revival today, we must first look back at the history of revivals in America. The United States has a rich heritage of spiritual awakenings that have shaped its cultural, social, and political landscape. These revivals have often come during times of moral decline and spiritual apathy, breathing new life into churches and communities.

One of the earliest and most significant revivals in American history was the First Great Awakening, which swept through the American colonies in the 1730s and 1740s. This movement was marked by powerful preaching from figures like Jonathan Edwards and George Whitefield, who emphasized personal repentance, the sovereignty of God, and the necessity of a personal relationship with Jesus Christ.

The First Great Awakening not only revived the church but also laid the groundwork for the American Revolution by promoting ideas of equality, liberty, and individual responsibility.

Jonathan Edwards, a prominent theologian and preacher, played a crucial role in the Awakening with his vivid sermons that emphasized the sovereignty of God, the depravity of mankind, and the necessity of personal conversion. His famous sermon, "Sinners in the Hands of an Angry God," vividly depicted the horrors of Hell and the urgent need for redemption, sparking intense emotional responses from his listeners.

George Whitefield, an itinerant preacher from England, further fueled the revival with his powerful oratory and dramatic preaching style. Whitefield traveled extensively, preaching to massive crowds in open fields and churches, often drawing thousands of people. His messages emphasized the need for a new birth, urging individuals to experience a personal, transformative relationship with Christ.

The First Great Awakening had significant social and cultural impacts. It broke down barriers within the Church, encouraging the formation of new denominations. The revival fostered a sense of a shared American identity among the colonists, contributing to a spirit of independence and unity that would later play a role in the American Revolution. It also challenged the established religious order, empowering ordinary individuals to question traditional authorities and seek a direct, personal connection with God.

The First Great Awakening was a pivotal event in American history, shaping the nation's religious life and laying the groundwork for future religious movements. It underscored the power of revival and the enduring impact of fervent preaching.

The Second Great Awakening, which began in the late 18th century and continued into the early 19th century, further solidified the role of revival in American life. This period was characterized by large "camp meetings," fiery sermons, and widespread conversions. It also had a profound social impact, leading to the growth of the abolitionist movement, the "temperance societies," and other social reforms. Key figures like Charles Finney played a crucial role in this revival, emphasizing the importance of human agency in responding to God's call and the need for societal change.

Central to the Second Great Awakening were "camp meetings," large outdoor religious gatherings where thousands of people would come to hear traveling preachers. Finney, one of the most influential preachers of this period, utilized a powerful and direct preaching style that emphasized personal salvation and societal reform. He believed that revival was not just a spontaneous act of God but could be fostered through human effort and organization.

The movement was marked by its emphasis on personal piety and a direct, emotional connection with God. This led to a surge in church membership and the establishment of new denominations.

The Second Great Awakening had profound social and cultural impacts. It played a crucial role in the temperance movement, which sought to reduce alcohol consumption, and the abolitionist movement, which aimed to end slavery. Women, in particular, found new opportunities for leadership within the Church and in social reform movements, as they were encouraged to take active roles in promoting moral and societal change.

Additionally, the revival emphasized the idea of a kind, loving God who desired the salvation of all people. The Second Great Awakening was a dynamic and transformative period in American religious history. It fostered a spirit of spiritual zeal, moral reform, and social activism that left a lasting legacy on the nation's religious and cultural landscape.

In the late 19th and early 20th centuries, the Third Great Awakening brought about another wave of spiritual renewal. This period saw the rise of the Social Gospel movement, which sought to apply Christian principles to social issues such as poverty, labor rights, and education.

Evangelists like Dwight L. Moody and Billy Sunday drew large crowds, calling for personal conversion and societal reform.

In 1906, America saw the Azusa Street Revival, which lasted until 1915. Beginning in Los Angeles, California, The Azusa Street Revival stands as a cornerstone in the history of modern Pentecostalism. This extraordinary outpouring of the Holy Spirit, marked by speaking in tongues, miraculous healings, and interracial unity, was spearheaded by African American preacher William J. Seymour.

Seymour, the son of former slaves, had encountered the teachings of Charles Parham on the baptism of the Holy Spirit and the evidence of speaking in tongues. His desire to experience and share this Pentecostal blessing led him to a small mission at 312 Azusa Street, where revival soon broke out. What began as a humble prayer meeting quickly escalated into a powerful movement, drawing people from all walks of life and ethnic backgrounds.

The meetings at Azusa Street were characterized by fervent prayer, passionate worship, and spontaneous manifestations of the Holy Spirit. Participants reported miraculous healings, prophecies, and a profound sense of God's presence. The revival's hallmark was the restoration of the gifts of the Holy Spirit, reminiscent of the events in the Book of Acts. Seymour's emphasis on humility, holiness, and unity set the tone for the gatherings, which often lasted for hours and drew crowds from across the globe.

One of the most remarkable aspects of the Azusa Street Revival was its inclusivity. In a deeply segregated society, the revival saw people of many races and backgrounds worshiping together. This interracial harmony, though criticized by many at the time, was a powerful testament to the unifying work of the Holy Spirit.

The impact of the Azusa Street Revival was profound and far-reaching. It birthed the global Pentecostal movement, which today numbers over 500 million adherents. Denominations such as the Assemblies of God, the Church of God in Christ, and the Foursquare Church trace their roots to this revival. The emphasis on Spirit baptism, spiritual gifts, and evangelism continues to shape the practices and theology of Pentecostal and charismatic churches worldwide.

The legacy of the Azusa Street Revival endures as a testament to the transformative power of the Holy Spirit, breaking down racial barriers, igniting a passion for evangelism, and restoring the dynamic gifts of the early church. It remains a pivotal moment in Christian history, demonstrating the profound impact of a community wholly surrendered to God's purposes.

More recently, the mid-20th century witnessed the emergence of the evangelical movement, with figures like Billy Graham leading massive crusades that reached millions with the message of the gospel.

The Jesus People Movement of the 1960s and 1970s marked a significant revival within the evangelical landscape, often characterized by its countercultural embrace and radical devotion to Christ. This revival emerged against a backdrop of social upheaval, with disillusioned youth seeking truth and meaning beyond the materialism and moral relativism prevalent at the time.

Central to this movement was Chuck Smith, the founder of Calvary Chapel in Costa Mesa, California, whose story was told in the 2023 movie, *Jesus Revolution*. Smith's approach was revolutionary; he opened his church doors to hippies, surfers, and the marginalized, offering them a message of hope and redemption through Jesus Christ. This inclusivity was counter to the traditional church's often rigid boundaries, resonating deeply with a generation yearning for authenticity and acceptance.

Smith's expository preaching, which thoroughly taught the Bible, provided a solid foundation for new believers. His emphasis on the authority of Scripture and the need for personal repentance and faith in Jesus attracted thousands. Under his leadership, Calvary Chapel grew exponentially, becoming a hub for the Jesus People Movement. The church's informal worship style, contemporary Christian music, and emphasis on community reflected the cultural milieu of the 70s, making the gospel accessible and relatable.

Other notable pastors emerged from Calvary Chapel, further spreading the movement's influence. Greg Laurie, who started as a young preacher under Smith's mentorship, became a prominent evangelist and founded Harvest Christian Fellowship. Laurie's Harvest Crusades have reached millions, continuing the work of evangelism and revival. Mike MacIntosh, who founded Horizon Christian Fellowship in San Diego, and Raul Ries, pastor of Calvary Chapel Golden Springs, also played significant roles in expanding the reach of the Jesus People Movement.

The impact of the Jesus People Movement extended far beyond Calvary Chapel. It sparked a nationwide revival, influencing countless churches and leading to the birth of the contemporary Christian music scene. Its legacy persists today in the ongoing vitality of Calvary Chapel and other ministries that trace their roots to this revival. The Jesus People Movement exemplifies how God's Spirit can move powerfully in unexpected ways, drawing diverse individuals to the transformative love of Jesus Christ.

These historical revivals share common elements: a recognition of spiritual decline, a call to repentance, fervent prayer, powerful preaching, and a resulting transformation of individuals and society. They remind us that revival is not just a distant memory but something we need today, perhaps more than ever before, for the Church and the nation.

II Chronicles 7:14 A Basis for Revival

Revival—a spiritual awakening that ignites hearts, transforms communities, and restores nations—is not just a distant hope but a divine promise deeply rooted in God's desire for His people. Throughout history, God has consistently demonstrated His faithfulness in responding to sincere cries for revival. The question that remains pertinent today is not whether God desires revival for America, but rather, whether His people will earnestly seek Him for it.

In the Bible, 2 Chronicles 7:14 lays out a clear blueprint for revival: "[If] My people who are called by My name humble themselves, and pray and seek My face, and turn from their wicked ways, then I will hear from Heaven, and I will forgive their sin and will heal their land." This verse encapsulates the divine invitation and conditional promise upon which revival hinges. It starts with God's people—those who profess faith in Him—taking intentional steps towards spiritual renewal.

First and foremost, revival necessitates a return to God—a turning away from worldly pursuits and a wholehearted pursuit of Him. The apostle John admonishes believers in 1 John 2:15-17 to "not love the world nor the things in the world... The world is passing away and also its lusts; but the one who does the will of God continues to live forever." This call to detachment from worldly allurements underscores the need for a radical reorientation of priorities among God's people. Revival demands a genuine love for God above all else, a love that permeates every aspect of life and ministry.

Furthermore, revival is birthed in prayer—persistent, fervent, and faith-filled prayer. James 5:16 assures us, "Therefore, confess your sins to one another, and pray for one another so that you may be healed. A prayer of a righteous person, when it is brought about, can accomplish much." Through prayer, believers align their hearts with God's purposes, interceding for personal and communal revival. Prayer cultivates intimacy with God, deepens dependence on His guidance, and invites His transforming presence into individual lives and across the nation.

Central to the call for revival is repentance—a heartfelt acknowledgment and turning away from sin. Psalm 51:10 records David's plea for renewal: "Create in me a clean heart, God, and renew a steadfast spirit within me." Genuine repentance involves a sincere confession of sins, a willingness to forsake wrongdoing, and a commitment to live in accordance with God's Word. It is through repentance that barriers are removed, relationships are restored, and spiritual vitality is renewed.

The Church, as the Body of Christ, plays a pivotal role in ushering in revival. This requires a return to biblical truth, uncompromising adherence to God's Word, and courageous proclamation of the gospel. Revelation 2:4-5 admonishes the church in Ephesus to "remember from where you have fallen, and repent, and do the deeds you did at first," emphasizing the importance of rediscovering and rekindling the fervent love for Christ that initially characterized the early church.

Revival in America hinges on the collective response of God's people—a unified, relentless pursuit of God's presence and His will. It requires humility to acknowledge our spiritual neediness, faith to believe in God's promises, and obedience to follow His lead. It demands a commitment to holiness, a dedication to prayer, and a fervent passion for evangelism and discipleship.

God's desire for revival in America is undeniably clear, and His promises are unwavering and eternal. However, the realization of revival depends upon the response of His people. Will we heed His call to humility, prayer, repentance, and wholehearted devotion? Will we abandon the temporary pleasures of this world and pursue a deeper relationship with Him? The choice lies with each believer—whether to embrace God's invitation to revival and become vessels through which His transformative power can flow into our churches, communities, and nation. As we cry out to God for revival, may we experience His grace, witness His restoration, and see His Kingdom come on earth as it is in Heaven.

In the pursuit of spiritual renewal and national revival, certain biblical passages stand as beacons of hope and guidance. Among them, II Chronicles 7:14 serves as a foundational scripture that encapsulates God's promise of restoration and renewal through repentance and prayer. This preface seeks to explore and unpack the profound truths embedded in this verse, drawing insights from Hebrew understanding, historical context, and perspectives from evangelical biblical scholars. I will mention the passage quite a bit in this book, so let's take a deeper look at it.

II Chronicles 7:14 A Translation and Contextual Analysis

"[If] My people who are called by My name humble themselves, and pray and seek My face, and turn from their wicked ways, then I will hear from Heaven, and I will forgive their sin and will heal their land." (NASB)

Hebrew Insights

The Hebrew language provides nuances that deepen our understanding of this verse:

Humble themselves (yit'ḥanəpʿū): This phrase implies a deliberate act of humility and contrition before God, acknowledging His sovereignty and our dependence on Him alone for restoration.

Pray (wəyiṯpalleʿū): Prayer is not merely a petition but a fervent cry to God, seeking His intervention and guidance in humility and faith.

Seek my face (wəyiḇaḏərū pānay): This phrase denotes a personal and intimate pursuit of God's presence and favor, desiring communion with Him above all else.

Turn from their wicked ways (wəyišəḇû mišəḇōtêhā): True repentance involves a genuine turning away from sin and disobedience, aligning one's life with God's righteous standards.

Historical Context

II Chronicles 7:14 was originally spoken to King Solomon after the completion of the temple in Jerusalem. The context includes God's response to Solomon's prayer of dedication and His covenant to bless or discipline Israel based on their faithfulness to Him (II Chronicles 7:12-22). The conditions outlined in verse 14 serve as a blueprint for God's people to experience His forgiveness, healing, and restoration.

Identification: "My people who are called by My name" refers to those who belong to God through a covenant relationship, identifying themselves with His character and purpose.

Humility: The call to humble oneself signifies recognizing one's spiritual poverty and dependency on God, setting aside pride and self-sufficiency.

Prayer and Seeking God's Face: These actions emphasize the importance of intimate communion with God, earnestly seeking His will and guidance through persistent prayer.

Repentance: Turning from wicked ways involves genuine sorrow for sin, accompanied by a deliberate turning toward righteousness and obedience to God's commands.

Application to Personal and National Revival

II Chronicles 7:14 provides a clear roadmap for both personal spiritual renewal and national revival.

Personal Revival: Individuals are called to humble themselves before God, confessing their sins and seeking His forgiveness through earnest prayer and repentance. This involves a deepening intimacy with God, a commitment to living in obedience to His Word, and a desire for personal holiness and spiritual growth.

National Revival: As a nation, revival begins with God's people collectively humbling themselves, praying fervently, seeking His face, and turning from sinful ways. This corporate repentance creates an environment where God's healing and restoration can flow, transforming communities, cultures, and societal structures.

II Chronicles 7:14 stands as a timeless promise *and* invitation from God—a promise of forgiveness, healing, and restoration for those who humbly seek Him in repentance and prayer. As we delve into the depths of this scripture, exploring its Hebrew roots, historical context, and evangelical perspectives, may we be inspired to embrace its principles wholeheartedly. May this serve as a catalyst for personal spiritual renewal and a clarion call for national revival, trusting in God's faithfulness to hear, forgive, and heal as we seek His face and turn toward Him with contrite hearts.

Purpose and Goals of This Book

The Coming American Revival is written with a sense of urgency and hope. It is a call to action for Christians to seek God with renewed passion, to pray fervently for revival, and to engage actively in the transformation of their communities and nation. The purpose of this book is threefold:

To Inspire a Vision for Revival: By examining the historical context of revivals in America and understanding the current state of our culture, we hope to inspire a vision for what God can do in our time. We will look at the characteristics of past revivals and draw lessons for today, recognizing that revival is not just a historical phenomenon but a present and future possibility.

To Equip Believers for Revival: Revival begins with individual believers and local churches. This book aims to equip Christians with practical tools and strategies for fostering revival in their own lives, families, churches, and communities. We will explore the foundational elements of revival, such as prayer, repentance, preaching, and discipleship, and provide practical steps for implementing these in daily life.

To Mobilize the Church for Action: Revival is not just about personal renewal; it is also about societal transformation. This book will challenge and encourage the Church to engage actively in the public square, addressing social issues from a biblical perspective and seeking to bring about positive change in every sphere of life. We will look at the role of Christians in education, the marketplace, government, and culture, and highlight examples of individuals and organizations making a difference.

As we embark on this journey together, let us remember that revival is ultimately a work of God. It is not something we can manufacture or manipulate, but something we can prepare for and participate in. Our role is to seek God earnestly, to humble ourselves in repentance, and to pray with faith and expectancy. If we do so, we can trust that God will honor His promises and bring about a revival that will transform our lives, our churches, and our nation.

In the pages that follow, we will delve deeper into the history of revivals, the current challenges we face, and the practical steps we can take to prepare for the coming American revival. May this book serve as a catalyst for a fresh outpouring of God's Spirit, igniting a passion for His glory and a longing for His Kingdom to come on earth as it is in Heaven.

Introduction

Psalm 85:6 (NASB): "Will You not revive us again, so that Your people may rejoice in You?"

Revival—a word that stirs the soul and ignites the spirit. Its etymology traces back to the Latin *revivere*, meaning "to live again." Revival, in the Christian context, signifies a spiritual reawakening from a state of dormancy or stagnation in the life of a believer or a church. It involves the rekindling of a vibrant relationship with God, marked by renewed faith, fervent prayer, and a passionate commitment to Christ and His mission. Revival is a divine visitation, a sovereign move of God that brings about deep conviction of sin, genuine repentance, and a profound transformation of lives and communities.

Revival is more than a series of meetings or an emotional response; it is a profound encounter with the living God that results in lasting change. Revival begins with a recognition of our spiritual need, a turning away from sin, and a turning toward God with all our hearts. It is characterized by a renewed love for God, a hunger for His Word, and a desire to live in obedience to His will. Revival restores the joy of salvation, rekindles the fire of evangelism, and renews the commitment to holiness and godly living.

The benefits of revival are many. At its core, revival brings a renewed sense of God's presence and power. Believers experience a deeper intimacy with God, a greater sensitivity to the leading of the Holy Spirit, and an increased capacity to love and serve others. Churches are revitalized, becoming vibrant communities of faith where lives are transformed, relationships are restored, families are blessed, and the gospel is proclaimed with boldness. Revival leads to greater unity among believers, breaking down barriers of division and fostering a spirit of cooperation and mutual support. Revival brings forgiveness, unity, love, and joy to those who experience it.

Revival also has a profound impact on society. When a church is revived, it becomes a powerful force for good in the world. Social ills are addressed, injustice is confronted, and communities are transformed. The church is viewed as a blessing to the community. Revival often leads to moral and ethical renewal, as individuals and communities turn away from sinful practices and embrace godly values. The light of Christ shines brightly in a revived church, illuminating the darkness and drawing others to the hope and salvation found in Jesus.

In the context of America, revival is our only hope. As a nation founded on principles derived from a relationship with God, America needs an awakening that will restore its moral and spiritual foundations. Our country is facing a myriad of challenges, such as moral decay, social unrest, political division, and spiritual apathy. These challenges cannot be solved by politics alone; they require a profound spiritual solution. Without revival, political efforts are bound to fail, as true and lasting change begins in the heart and flows out to every sphere of society. We can be involved in politics, but politics is not the answer to saving America. A politician cannot save America. Only God can save America. Christians who put their hope in a political figure alone will always be greatly disappointed.

To experience revival, America must return to the foundational principles upon which it was built. This involves a collective recognition of our spiritual needs and a heartfelt turning to God in repentance and faith. Prayer is the key to revival. As individuals and churches commit to fervent and persistent prayer, seeking God's face and interceding for our nation, we create an environment where the Holy Spirit can move powerfully.

Repentance is another crucial element of revival. We must turn away from sin and embrace a life of holiness and obedience to God's Word. Unfortunately, the Church is filled with Christians who have not yet turned their lives over to the full sanctification of God. They are justified, but not sanctified. In fact, when you look at the average Christian's life, you will find that it looks almost exactly like the average non-Christian's life, except for their church attendance. That is a problem. We are worldly.

Because of this, the faithful preaching and teaching of God's Word are essential for revival. The Church must boldly proclaim the gospel, calling people to repentance and faith in Jesus Christ. Revival often begins with a renewed emphasis on the authority and sufficiency of Scripture, as believers immerse themselves in God's Word and allow it to transform their lives.

In addition to prayer, repentance, and the preaching of God's Word, unity and community within the Church are vital for revival. Jesus prayed for the unity of His followers, recognizing that unity is a powerful witness to the world. When the Church is united in love and purpose, it creates a fertile ground for revival. Authentic community, characterized by mutual support, accountability, and a commitment to one another's spiritual growth, helps to sustain revival and extend its impact. Think about it. When you ask someone why they don't believe in Jesus or go to church, one of the most common questions in response is, "If Christianity is true, why are there so many denominations?" The world is watching and when they see us fighting and separating over petty issues, they are not given to belief. Revival brings unity. Not conformity, as we still have our differences, but unity—togetherness in spite of our differences.

Social engagement and outreach are also critical components of revival. A revived church will naturally turn its attention outward, seeking to meet the needs of the community and share the love of Christ. Evangelism, discipleship, and social action are all part of a church's mission and contribute to the broader impact of revival on society. Think about it, the last two things Jesus left us with are two passages that command us to be witnesses!

Matthew 28:18-20 (NASB): "And Jesus came up and spoke to them, saying, 'All authority in Heaven and on earth has been given to Me. Go, therefore, and make disciples of all the nations, baptizing them in the name of the Father and the Son and the Holy Spirit, teaching them to follow all that I commanded you; and behold, I am with you always, to the end of the age.'"

Acts 1:8 (NASB): "But you will receive power when the Holy Spirit has come upon you; and you shall be My witnesses both in Jerusalem and in all Judea, and Samaria, and as far as the remotest part of the earth."

Revival, therefore, is not just a spiritual experience for individuals; it is a movement that transforms the Church and impacts the world. It brings about a profound and lasting change that restores, renews, and revitalizes every aspect of life. As America seeks revival, we must recognize that it is not something we can manufacture or control; it is a sovereign work of God. Our role is to prepare the way through prayer, repentance, and obedience, trusting that God, in His mercy and grace, will pour out His Spirit and bring about a mighty revival in our land.

Revival is our only hope for a transformed America. It is the means by which God restores His people, revitalizes His Church, and renews society. Without revival, political efforts and human solutions will fall short. But with revival, we can experience the fullness of God's presence, power, and purpose in our lives and our nation. As we seek God for revival, let us do so with humility, faith, and a commitment to His mission, believing that He will answer our prayers and bring about a great awakening that will impact generations to come.

Chapter One
Understanding Revival

Definition and Characteristics of Revival

Revival, in its most profound sense, is a sovereign work of God that brings about a deep and lasting transformation in individuals and communities. It is a powerful awakening that rekindles spiritual fervor, renews faith, and restores a sense of God's presence and purpose. Revival is not merely an emotional experience or a temporary enthusiasm; it is a profound encounter with the living God that leads to genuine repentance, holiness, and a renewed commitment to His will.

The characteristics of revival include:

Deep Conviction of Sin: Revival often begins with a profound awareness of sin and heartfelt sorrow for having offended a holy God. This conviction leads to genuine repentance and a turn away from sinful practices. Christians come to a place where they can no longer live with the sin they have allowed to creep into their lives. They have a desire to be holy and repent of their sin. People become aware of their sins, sins they have never seen before, and they are convinced to stop their sinful behavior. There is a deep contrition that comes over them, driving them to change their lives.

Intense Prayer: Prayer is both a precursor and a hallmark of revival. During revival, individuals and congregations engage in fervent and persistent prayer, seeking God's face and pleading for His mercy and intervention. The revived Christian craves time with the Lord. They desire to be in His presence and to speak to Him and hear from Him.

They feel compelled to enter into the presence of the Lord as often as possible.

Powerful Preaching: Revival is marked by the preaching of God's Word with boldness, clarity, and power. The Holy Spirit anoints the preaching, making it deeply convicting and transformative. One of the great travesties in America today is the nearly complete absence of powerful Biblical preaching. We need pastors and teachers who are dedicated to this charge that Paul gave the young pastor, Timothy,

> I solemnly exhort you in the presence of God and of Christ Jesus, who is to judge the living and the dead, and by His appearing and His Kingdom: preach the Word; be ready in season and out of season; correct, rebuke, and exhort, with great patience and instruction. For the time will come when they will not tolerate sound doctrine; but wanting to have their ears tickled, they will accumulate for themselves teachers in accordance with their own desires, and they will turn their ears away from the truth and will turn aside to myths. (II Timothy 4:1-4)

Renewed Worship: Worship during revival is characterized by a sense of awe, reverence, and joy in the presence of God. There is a fresh outpouring of praise and adoration, often accompanied by a spontaneous and heartfelt expression of love for God. I have often heard people say, "I can't imagine that all we will do in Heaven is worship." When we are revived and come face-to-face with the living God, we will completely understand the desire to worship!

The problem with our American churches is that you rarely see true worship in any of them. What you see in most churches today are singalongs. I like the idea of a wide variety of musical types in our churches. If you enjoy old hymns, that is great. I feel the same about modern music as well. Different people enjoy different styles. What I am talking about is about the heart of worship. Standing in a large group - even at a church - is not worship in and of itself. No, true worship comes through a devoted heart directed toward the Lord. Rote repetition is not true worship, per se, whether it is liturgical sayings or the "sing the verse seventeen times in a row" style of modern "worship" songs. Any music can be an expression of worship, if the heart of the individual is in it, while if the heart isn't in it, even the most spiritual song ever written would not be worship.

Changed Lives: Genuine revival results in visible changes in the lives of individuals. There is a renewed commitment to holiness, integrity, and obedience to God's Word. Relationships are restored, and there is a new zeal for evangelism and service. The revived Christian will see actual changes in their thoughts, words, and actions. They will know deeply the truths of Romans 12:1-2,

> Therefore I urge you, brothers and sisters, by the mercies of God, to present your bodies as a living and holy sacrifice, acceptable to God, which is your spiritual service of worship. And do not be conformed to this world, but be transformed by the renewing of your mind, so that you may prove what the will of God is, that which is good and acceptable and perfect.

Community Impact: Revival extends beyond the Church, impacting the broader community. Social structures are influenced, injustices are addressed, and there is a noticeable improvement in moral and ethical standards. Revival is not something that stays inside the walls of the church. True revival will always spill over into the community, blessing those who come in contact with those who have been filled with the Holy Spirit.

Biblical Examples of Revival

The Bible provides numerous examples of revival, illustrating how God has worked throughout history to restore His people and advance His Kingdom.

The Revival Under King Josiah (2 Kings 22-23): King Josiah's reign was marked by a significant revival in Judah. After discovering the Book of the Law in the temple, Josiah was deeply convicted of the nation's sin. He led the people in repentance, destroyed idols, and renewed their covenant with God. This revival brought about a sweeping reform, turning the nation back to God.

The Revival Under Nehemiah, a high official of the Persian court (Nehemiah 8-10): After returning from exile, Nehemiah led the rebuilding of Jerusalem's walls. During this time, Ezra the Scribe read the Law to the people, leading to a powerful revival. The people wept, confessed their sins, and renewed their commitment to follow God's commands. This revival brought about a profound spiritual renewal and a renewed dedication to God's covenant.

Pentecost (Acts 2): The outpouring of the Holy Spirit at Pentecost marked the beginning of the Christian Church. The disciples were filled with the Holy Spirit, and Peter's powerful preaching led to the conversion of 3,000 people in a single day. This revival continued to spread, transforming lives and establishing the early church as a vibrant, Spirit-filled community.

Signs of the Need for Revival

As we consider the current state of American culture and spirituality, it becomes evident that there are several signs indicating the *urgent* need for revival.

Decline in Church Attendance and Engagement: One of the most alarming signs is the decline in church attendance and engagement. According to recent studies, church membership and attendance have been steadily declining in the United States for several decades. Fewer people identify as Christians, and more identify as religiously unaffiliated, often referred to as "nones." This trend is particularly pronounced among younger generations, who are increasingly skeptical of organized religion and traditional Christian beliefs.

Here is the weekly church attendance over time in America according to (PEW Research Center):

1950's - 49%
1970's - 40%
1990's - 36%
2023 - 31%

This decline in church participation has significant implications for the spiritual health of individuals and communities. When people disengage from the church, they miss out on the support, accountability, and spiritual nourishment that comes from being part of a faith community. The decline in church attendance also weakens the church's influence in society, as its voice becomes less prominent and its impact diminishes.

Some today say, "Well, you know, we don't need to go to church to be a Christian." This is true. But you do need to go to church to be an obedient Christian. Consider Hebrews 10:23-25,

> Let's hold firmly to the confession of our hope without wavering, for He who promised is faithful; and let's consider how to encourage one another in love and good deeds, not abandoning our own meeting together, as is the habit of some people, but encouraging one another; and all the more as you see the day drawing near.

Moral and Ethical Challenges in Society: The moral and ethical challenges facing American society today are another clear sign of the need for revival. Issues such as abortion, same-sex marriage, and gender identity have become flashpoints in the culture wars, reflecting a departure from traditional Christian teachings. Moral relativism and secularism have gained ground, leading to a society where absolute truth is questioned, and individual autonomy is elevated above all else.

These moral and ethical challenges are not just abstract issues; they have real and profound impacts on individuals and communities. The breakdown of traditional family structures and the prevalence of both addiction and mental health issues are all symptoms of a society that has strayed from God's standards. In this context, revival is desperately needed to restore a sense of moral clarity, compassion, and justice.

Spiritual Apathy Among Christians: Perhaps the most concerning sign of the need for revival is the spiritual apathy that pervades much of the Church today. Many Christians are content with a superficial faith that lacks depth, commitment, and transformative power. Prayer and Bible reading are often neglected, and the pursuit of holiness and personal discipleship is overshadowed by the distractions and demands of modern life and the allure of sin.

This spiritual apathy is evident in the lack of passion and zeal for God, the absence of a sense of urgency for evangelism and mission, and the prevalence of compromise and complacency. The Church has, in many ways, become lukewarm, losing its prophetic voice and its impact on the surrounding culture. In this context, revival is needed to awaken believers to the reality of God's presence, the urgency of His mission, and the power of His Spirit. I use the word lukewarm purposefully because it reminds us of how God feels about those who are lukewarm. In Revelation 3 we see a rebuke given to the church of Laodicea,

> He who has the seven spirits of God and the seven stars, says this: 'I know your deeds, that you have a name that you are alive, and yet you are dead. Be constantly alert, and strengthen the things that remain, which were about to die; for I have not found your deeds completed in the sight of My God. So remember what you have received and heard; and keep it, and repent. Then if you are not alert, I will come like a thief, and you will not know at what hour I will come to you. But you have a few people in Sardis who have not soiled their garments; and they will walk with Me in white,

for they are worthy. The one who overcomes will be clothed the same way, in white garments; and I will not erase his name from the book of life, and I will confess his name before My Father and before His angels. The one who has an ear, let him hear what the Spirit says to the churches.' (Revelation 3:1-6)

Sound like anyone you know?

Looking Forward

Understanding revival is crucial as we seek to address the spiritual, moral, and social challenges facing America today. Revival is a sovereign work of God that brings about a deep and lasting transformation, characterized by repentance of sin, intense prayer, powerful preaching, renewed worship, changed lives, and community impact. The Bible provides numerous examples of revival, and history shows us that revival has had a profound impact on society.

The key elements of genuine revival include prayer and repentance; the preaching of God's Word; the work of the Holy Spirit; commitment to holiness, unity, and community; and evangelism and mission. These elements provide a blueprint for seeking and experiencing revival in our own time.

The signs of the need for revival are evident in the decline in church attendance and engagement, the moral and ethical challenges in society, and the spiritual apathy among Christians. In light of these signs, the call to revival is urgent and compelling.

As we move forward in this book, let us seek God with renewed passion, pray fervently for revival, and engage actively in the transformation of our communities and nation. May God, in His mercy and grace, bring about a revival that will renew our faith, restore our hope, and advance His Kingdom for His glory and our good.

Chapter Two
The Foundations of Revival

Revival is a powerful work of God that brings about profound spiritual transformation in individuals and communities. To understand how revival can be sparked and sustained, we must examine its foundations: prayer, repentance, and the preaching of the Word of God. These elements are crucial in creating an environment where the Holy Spirit can move powerfully, bringing about lasting change and renewal.

Prayer and Repentance: The Importance of Personal and Corporate Prayer

Prayer is the lifeblood of revival. It is through prayer that believers communicate with God, express their dependence on Him, and seek His guidance and intervention. Both personal and corporate prayer are essential in laying the groundwork for revival.

Personal Prayer: Personal prayer is the intimate communication between an individual and God. It is a time of pouring out one's heart, confessing one's sins, seeking God's will, and interceding for others. Personal prayer cultivates a deep relationship with God, allowing individuals to align their hearts with His purposes. The Bible is filled with examples of personal prayer that led to significant spiritual breakthroughs. For instance, Daniel's commitment to personal prayer, even in the face of persecution, resulted in God's favor and protection (Daniel 6).

Corporate Prayer: Corporate prayer involves the collective intercession of a community of believers. It is a powerful expression of unity and dependence on God. Matthew 18:19-20 says, "Again I say to you, that if two of you agree on earth about anything that they may ask, it shall be done for them by My Father who is in Heaven. For where two or three have gathered together in My name, I am there in their midst." When believers come together to pray, their collective faith and fervor create an atmosphere where the Holy Spirit can move mightily. The early church in Acts provides a compelling example of the power of corporate prayer. After Jesus' ascension, the disciples gathered together in one place, praying fervently. This united prayer preceded the outpouring of the Holy Spirit at Pentecost, which marked the birth of the Church (Acts 2).

One of the great tragedies of the American church is the emptiness of our prayer rooms and the lack of Christians who truly develop a prayer life. Throw a church BBQ and they will line up out the door and into the parking lot. Hold a one-hour night of prayer and there will be less than ten people. This is the weak and ineffective modern church.

The Synergy of Personal and Corporate Prayer: Both personal and corporate prayer are essential for revival. Personal prayer deepens individual believers' relationship with God, while corporate prayer fosters a sense of unity and collective purpose. Together they create a powerful synergy that invites God's presence and power into the lives of individuals and communities.

In order to see revival in America, we need both personal and corporate prayer to take their rightful places in the priorities of Christians and churches.

A Biblical Call to Repentance

Repentance is another foundational element of revival. It is a heartfelt acknowledgment of sin, accompanied by a sincere turn away from sinful behaviors and toward God. The Bible consistently calls God's people to repentance as a prerequisite for experiencing His favor and blessing.

The simple question that must confront every single Christian is this: are you repentant?

Until the Christians in America become so, revival will be only a dream.

Old Testament Examples of Repentance: The Old Testament is replete with calls for repentance. The prophets repeatedly called for Israel to turn from its wicked ways and return to God. For example, the prophet Joel called for the people to "return to the Lord your God, for He is gracious and compassionate, slow to anger, abounding in mercy and relenting of catastrophe." (Joel 2:13). Listen to the repentant heart of David when confronted by his affair with Bathsheba in Psalm 51,

> Be gracious to me, God,
> according to Your faithfulness;
> According to the greatness of Your compassion,
> wipe out my wrongdoings.
>
> Wash me thoroughly from my guilt
> And cleanse me from my sin.
> For I know my wrongdoings,
> And my sin is constantly before me.
>
> Against You, You only, I have sinned
> And done what is evil in Your sight,
> So that You are justified when You speak
> And blameless when You judge.
>
> Behold, I was brought forth in guilt,
> And in sin my mother conceived me.
> Behold, You desire truth in the innermost being,
> And in secret You will make wisdom known to me.
>
> Purify me with hyssop, and I will be clean;
> Cleanse me, and I will be whiter than snow.

Let me hear joy and gladness,
Let the bones You have broken rejoice.
Hide Your face from my sins
And wipe out all my guilty deeds.

Create in me a clean heart, God,
And renew a steadfast spirit within me.
Do not cast me away from Your presence,
And do not take Your Holy Spirit from me.
Restore to me the joy of Your salvation,
And sustain me with a willing spirit.
Then I will teach wrongdoers Your ways,
And sinners will be converted to You.

Save me from the guilt of bloodshed, God,
the God of my salvation;
Then my tongue will joyfully sing of Your
righteousness.

Lord, open my lips,
So that my mouth may declare Your praise.
For You do not delight in sacrifice,
otherwise I would give it;
You do not take pleasure in burnt offering.
The sacrifices of God are a broken spirit;
A broken and a contrite heart, God,
You will not despise.

By Your favor do good to Zion;
Build the walls of Jerusalem.
Then You will delight in righteous sacrifices,
In burnt offering and whole burnt offering;
Then bulls will be offered on Your altar.

New Testament Examples: The New Testament continues this theme.
John the Baptist's ministry was marked by a call to repentance,
"Repent, for the Kingdom of Heaven is at hand" (Matthew 3:2). Jesus

Himself began His public ministry with a call to repentance, "From that time Jesus began to preach and say, "Repent, for the Kingdom of Heaven is at hand" (Matthew 4:17). The apostles also emphasized the necessity of repentance in their preaching. Peter's sermon on the day of Pentecost culminated in a call to repentance, "Repent, and each of you be baptized in the name of Jesus Christ for the forgiveness of your sins; and you will receive the gift of the Holy Spirit" (Acts 2:38). In all, the words "repent" and "repentance" are used 53 times in the New Testament.

Preaching and the Word of God: The Power of Expository Preaching

Preaching is another foundational element of revival. Expository preaching, which involves the careful explanation and application of Scripture, plays a crucial role in bringing about spiritual renewal. It allows God's Word to speak directly to the hearts of listeners, convicting, encouraging, and transforming them.

Expository preaching involves a systematic and thorough exposition of biblical texts. The preacher seeks to uncover the original meaning of the passage, explain its context, and apply its timeless truths to contemporary life. This method ensures that the message is rooted in Scripture and that God's Word remains central to the preaching. Too many preachers today use the Bible only as a jumping off point to teach a more palatable Christian motivational speech.

Impact of Expository Preaching: Expository preaching has a profound impact on individuals and communities because it allows the power of God's Word to work effectively. Hebrews 4:12 declares, "For the Word of God is living and active, and sharper than any two-edged sword, even penetrating as far as the division of soul and spirit, of both joints and marrow, and able to judge the thoughts and intentions of the heart." When God's Word is preached faithfully, it penetrates hearts, convinces listeners of their sins, and brings about genuine transformation. The Word of God changes lives, the words of men do not.

Examples of Powerful Expository Preaching: Throughout history, expository preaching has played a pivotal role in sparking and sustaining revivals. During the Reformation, Martin Luther's expository preaching of the book of Romans led to a profound renewal of faith and a rediscovery of the gospel of grace. In the 18th century, Charles Spurgeon's expository sermons drew thousands to faith in Christ and revitalized the Church in England. In the 20th century, the preaching of Martyn Lloyd-Jones at Westminster Chapel in London brought about a deep spiritual awakening and a renewed hunger for God's Word.

The Role of Scripture in Personal and Societal Transformation

Scripture is the foundation of revival because it is through the Word of God that individuals and societies are transformed. The Bible is not just a collection of ancient writings, it is the living and active Word of God that has the power to change lives and shape cultures.

Personal Transformation: Scripture has the power to transform individuals by revealing God's character, convincing readers of sin, and guiding believers in righteous living. Psalm 19:7-8 declares, "The Law of the Lord is perfect, restoring the soul; the testimony of the Lord is sure, making wise the simple. The precepts of the Lord are right, rejoicing the heart; the commandment of the Lord is pure, enlightening the eyes." When individuals immerse themselves in God's Word, they experience a renewal of their minds and a transformation of their lives.

Societal Transformation: Scripture also has the power to transform societies by providing a moral and ethical framework for justice, compassion, and righteousness. The impact of the Bible on Western civilization is profound. The principles of human dignity, rule of law, and social justice are deeply rooted in biblical teachings. During times of revival, the influence of Scripture on society becomes even more pronounced, as communities embrace biblical values and seek to live according to God's standards. For example, God spoke through the Prophet Amos to tell the Israelites that their worship was worthless unless it produced justice and righteousness,I hate, I reject your festivals,

> Nor do I delight in your festive assemblies.

> Even though you offer up to Me burnt offerings and your grain offerings, I will not accept them;
> And I will not even look at the peace offerings of your fattened oxen.

> Take away from Me the noise of your songs;
> I will not even listen to the sound of your harps.

> But let justice roll out like waters,
> And righteousness like an ever-flowing stream. (Amos 5:21-24)

Examples of Societal Transformation through Scripture: The influence of Scripture on society is evident throughout history. The abolition of slavery in the 19th century was driven by a biblical understanding of human dignity and equality. Christian leaders like William Wilberforce and Harriet Beecher Stowe were inspired by their faith to fight for the rights of the oppressed. The Civil Rights Movement in the 20th century was also deeply rooted in biblical principles, with leaders like Martin Luther King Jr. drawing on Scripture to advocate for justice and equality.

Examples of Preaching that Led to Revival

Preaching has played a crucial role in many revivals throughout history. When God's Word is proclaimed with clarity, conviction, and power, it has the ability to ignite spiritual renewal and bring about lasting change. Romans 10:17 reminds us that "faith comes from hearing, and hearing by the Word of Christ."

Jonathan Edwards and the First Great Awakening: Jonathan Edwards was a key figure in the First Great Awakening in America. His preaching was marked by a deep commitment to Scripture and a powerful emphasis on the need for personal repentance and faith. His sermon "Sinners in the Hands of an Angry God" is one of the most famous examples of revival preaching. In this sermon, Edwards vividly described the reality of God's judgment and the urgency of turning to Christ for salvation. The sermon had a profound impact on his listeners, leading to widespread repentance and a powerful outpouring of the Holy Spirit.

George Whitefield and the Great Awakening: George Whitefield, a contemporary of Edwards, was another powerful preacher during the Great Awakening. His open-air preaching attracted thousands of listeners, and his messages were characterized by a passionate call to repentance and faith in Christ. Whitefield's preaching transcended denominational boundaries and sparked revival across the American colonies. His emphasis on the necessity of a personal relationship with Jesus Christ resonated deeply with his audiences, leading to a significant spiritual awakening.

Charles Finney and the Second Great Awakening: Charles Finney was a leading figure in the Second Great Awakening in the United States. His preaching was marked by an urgent call to repentance and a clear presentation of the gospel. Finney believed that revival was not a miraculous event but the result of the faithful preaching of God's Word and the response of repentant hearts. His revival meetings were characterized by intense emotional conviction and a strong emphasis on personal conversion. Finney's preaching led to widespread revivals in the northeastern United States, resulting in thousands of conversions and the establishment of new churches.

Billy Graham and the 20th Century Revivals: Billy Graham was one of the most influential evangelists of the 20th century. His preaching reached millions of people around the world through radio and television. Graham's messages were characterized by a clear and compelling presentation of the gospel, an urgent call to repentance, and a deep reliance on the power of the Holy Spirit. His ministry led to countless conversions and a renewed commitment to evangelism and discipleship in the church.

The foundations of revival are rooted in prayer, repentance, and the preaching of God's Word. Personal and corporate prayer create an environment where the Holy Spirit can move powerfully, bringing about spiritual renewal and transformation. Repentance is a crucial component of revival, as it involves a heartfelt turn away from sin and toward God. The preaching of God's Word, particularly through expository preaching, is essential in bringing about personal and societal transformation.

Throughout history, many revivals have been sparked by fervent prayer, heartfelt repentance, and powerful preaching. These elements are not just historical anecdotes; they are foundational principles that continue to be relevant today. As we seek revival in our own time, let us commit ourselves to prayer, repentance, and the faithful preaching of God's Word. May God, in His mercy and grace, bring about a revival that will renew our faith, restore our hope, and advance His Kingdom for His glory and our good.

Chapter Three
Revival in the Church

Revival begins in the hearts of individuals but must also transform the local church if it is to have a lasting and widespread impact. For a revival to take root and flourish, the local church must experience a profound renewal, characterized by a return to the core principles of the Christian faith. This chapter will explore the strategies for fostering revival in congregations, the role of leadership in revival, the importance of unity and community in the church, and the ways to mobilize the church for action through evangelism, discipleship, and social engagement.

Revitalizing Local Church Strategies for Fostering Revival in Congregations

To foster revival in congregations, it is essential to implement strategies that create an environment where the Holy Spirit can work powerfully. These strategies involve a combination of spiritual disciplines, practical steps, and a commitment to the mission of the church.

What you will notice as you read below is that this doesn't look like what the American church by and large looks like today. Instead, our churches feel like amusement parks. One friend I know goes to a mega church that the locals call, "Six Flags Over Jesus." That is an unfortunate term for a church to be known as. Other churches feel like a sporting event or a theatrical performance. The audience comes and watches what the performers do and say. They may even get up and sing along a bit or clap along, much like attendees of a sporting event would do "the wave." The true church, experiencing a revival, would look much more like this...

Prioritizing Prayer and Worship: Revival begins with a renewed focus on prayer and worship. Congregations must become houses of prayer, where members regularly gather to seek God's presence, intercede for one another, and pray for the outpouring of the Holy Spirit. Corporate worship should be vibrant, heartfelt, and centered on glorifying God. Worship services should provide opportunities for individuals to encounter God deeply, respond to His Word, and experience His transforming power. As it is, most Sunday mornings in church in America might better be described as "faith-based social gatherings." We drink coffee, see our friends, follow along through a few worship songs, and a short speech to make you feel good, utilizing a passage of the Bible or two. We need to begin to ask: What would happen if we actually focused on true prayer and worship?

Emphasizing Biblical Teaching and Preaching: The faithful preaching and teaching of God's Word are essential for revival. Expository preaching that explains and applies Scripture helps believers understand God's will and grow in their faith. Pastors and teachers should prioritize preaching the gospel, emphasizing the need for repentance, faith, and obedience. Bible studies, small groups, and discipleship classes should be offered to help believers grow in their knowledge of Scripture and apply its truths to their lives. For the vast majority of Christians in America today, almost all of their Christian experience revolves around Sunday morning service, which consists of a few short songs and a feel-good message. Is it of little surprise then that our people are weak, starved of true and powerful experiences and encounters with God?

Cultivating a Culture of Repentance and Holiness: A culture of repentance and holiness must be cultivated within the congregation. This involves creating an environment where individuals feel safe to confess their sins, seek forgiveness, and pursue holiness. Accountability groups, mentoring relationships, and pastoral care can support believers in their journey toward spiritual maturity. The church must also address areas of sin and compromise, calling its members to live lives that reflect the character of Christ. And we must preach about all sins mentioned in the scriptures, not just the ones we deem the most egregious. For example, greed is mentioned alongside homosexuality in a list of sins in I Corinthians 6:9-10, yet the typical evangelical church will gladly preach against homosexuality—as they should, of course—but neglect to speak against greed, which, almost for sure, has a deeper root in the average suburban church than homosexuality does.

Encouraging Personal and Corporate Revival: Personal revival precedes corporate revival. Congregations should encourage personal spiritual disciplines such as daily Bible reading, prayer, fasting, and personal worship. Testimonies of personal revival can inspire and encourage others to seek God more fervently. Additionally, special events such as revival meetings, retreats, and conferences can provide focused times for seeking God and experiencing His presence.

Fostering a Missional Mindset: Revival is not just for the benefit of the church but for the advancement of God's Kingdom. Congregations must develop a missional mindset, recognizing that they are called to be a light in their communities and beyond. This involves equipping and mobilizing members for evangelism, outreach, and social engagement. The church should seek to impact its community by meeting practical needs, sharing the gospel, and demonstrating Christ's love in tangible ways. Unfortunately, the average Christian today cannot speak one paragraph explaining the gospel in simple terms, understandable by the average person; they are thoroughly unequipped.

Role of Leadership in Revival

Leadership plays a crucial role in fostering and sustaining revival in the church. Pastors, elders, and ministry leaders must lead by example, demonstrating a deep commitment to prayer, holiness, and the mission of the church. Ephesians 4:12-13 reminds us that, "So Christ himself gave the apostles, the prophets, the evangelists, the pastors, and teachers, to equip His people for works of service, so that the Body of Christ may be built up..."

Leading by Example: Leaders must model the spiritual disciplines and behaviors they wish to see in their congregations. This includes maintaining a vibrant personal prayer life, regularly studying and applying Scripture, and pursuing personal holiness. Leaders should also be transparent about their own spiritual journeys, including their struggles and victories, to inspire and encourage others. All too often our churches are led by pastors whose spiritual life is as dead as their parishioners. Being a pastor is a job to them and they are dead inside. Our pastors and leaders need revival!

Preaching with Passion and Conviction: Pastors and preachers must proclaim God's Word with passion, conviction, and clarity. Their preaching should be rooted in Scripture, centered on the gospel, and aimed at transforming lives. Preaching that calls for repentance, faith, and obedience is essential for sparking revival. Leaders should also be sensitive to the leading of the Holy Spirit, allowing Him to guide their messages and ministry. American churches, many of whom were heavily influenced by the "church for the unchurched" model, do not preach the whole gospel. They preach a feel-good phony gospel that is no gospel at all. Revival pastors preach the whole of the gospel.

Creating a Culture of Prayer: Leaders must prioritize prayer in their own lives and the life of the church. This includes organizing regular prayer meetings, encouraging personal prayer, and fostering a culture where prayer is central to every aspect of church life. Leaders should also lead by example, participating in and leading corporate prayer times, and interceding for their congregation and community. This is perhaps the easiest way to prove where a church is in its relationship with God. In most American churches today, you can get half the congregation out for a movie night or a feel-good event but hold a prayer service and you get four or five people. That tells you right there what the spiritual state of a church is. People will follow their leaders. Church leaders must make it known that prayer meetings are important and that they hold a special place in the church and on the church calendar.

Equipping and Empowering Others: Revival is not a one-person endeavor; it requires the active participation of the entire congregation. Leaders should focus on equipping and empowering others for ministry. This involves identifying and developing spiritual gifts, providing training and resources, and creating opportunities for members to serve and lead. Empowering others helps to create a sense of ownership and involvement, which is crucial for sustaining revival. The great commission in Matthew 28 tells us that we are to make disciples. What most churches do, at best, is make converts. Many ministries stop after conversion and never disciple their people. This is why we have so many weak Christians in our churches. They know Jesus but they never go past that to a deeper relationship and walk with Christ.

Maintaining Vision and Focus: Leaders must maintain a clear vision and focus for the church. This includes articulating the mission and goals of the church, setting priorities, and keeping the congregation aligned with God's purposes. Leaders should regularly communicate the vision, celebrate progress, and address any distractions or obstacles that may hinder the church's mission. A clear vision helps to unite congregations and keep them motivated and focused on the work of His Kingdom.

One verse that many of you know is Proverbs 29:18. I want to show you two different translations that will show you some interesting nuances and things to think about:

"Where there is no revelation, people cast off restraint." NIV

"Where there is no vision, the people perish" KJV

I like combining these two translations because it shows what God is really trying to tell us. Here is what my paraphrase looks like...

Where there is no revealed vision of God, people will throw off their restraint and ultimately perish spiritually.

We need our leaders to give us God's vision so we can stay focused on Christ and thrive spiritually!

Importance of Unity and Community in the Church

Unity and community are vital components of revival. A divided church cannot effectively fulfill its mission or experience the fullness of God's blessing. Unity fosters an environment where the Holy Spirit can move freely, and the community provides the support and encouragement needed for spiritual growth. John 13:35 tells us that people will know we are Christians if we love one another. Instead of this, most people look at the church and ask why we are always fighting each other. Unity would go a long way as an evangelism method.

Promoting Unity: Unity in a church is achieved when members are united in their love for God and commitment to His purposes. Leaders must promote unity by addressing conflicts, fostering reconciliation, and encouraging mutual respect and love among members. Unity is strengthened when a church embraces diversity and recognizes that each member has a unique role to play in the Body of Christ. Ephesians 4:3 exhorts believers to "Make every effort to keep the unity of the Spirit through the bond of peace." I would also add that the churches in the community must show unity with one another. Again, unfortunately, this can be tough to get buy-in from pastors, who oftentimes see themselves in competition with the other pastors in town. What would happen if we communicated with, supported, and even rooted for the other churches in town? Now that would be powerful.

Building Authentic Community: An authentic community is characterized by genuine relationships, mutual support, and a commitment to one another's spiritual growth. Small groups, discipleship classes, and fellowship events can help build community by providing opportunities for members to connect, share their lives, and grow together.

The early church in Acts 2:42-47 provides a model of authentic community, where believers devoted themselves to the apostles' teaching, fellowship, breaking of bread, and prayer.

Encouraging Mutual Accountability: Mutual accountability is essential for spiritual growth and revival. When members hold one another accountable, they are more likely to stay committed to their spiritual disciplines and resist temptation. Accountability groups, mentoring relationships, and pastoral care can provide the support and encouragement needed for members to stay on track and grow in their faith. One of the downsides of modern culture is that when someone gets into something at a church, they merely leave and disappear, taking their issues to another church. When I was a pastor, if someone came to our church from another church in town, I always asked what the issue was. I would often also call the other pastor. If there were unresolved issues, I told them they were not welcome at our church until they dealt with those issues back at the other church. This is accountability.

I know of one pastor who, when one of his church members, a notable NFL player, committed a sin that made headlines, told the player that he would need to address his fellow church members to confess his sins and seek forgiveness. And guess what? That player stood in front of the congregation. He repented and asked his fellow Christians to forgive him for hurting the reputation of Christ and their congregation, and they did. They embraced him in his repentance. That is how it should work. This is almost unimaginable in today's church, but that is exactly the kind of accountability our churches need to demonstrate.

Serving One Another: Serving one another is a tangible expression of love and unity. When members use their gifts and talents to serve the church and community, they demonstrate the love of Christ and build up the Body of Christ. Leaders should encourage and provide opportunities for members to serve, recognizing that service is an essential aspect of discipleship and spiritual growth.

Celebrating Milestones and Victories: Celebrating milestones and victories helps to build unity and foster a sense of community. Recognizing and celebrating spiritual growth, answered prayers, and ministry achievements encourages members and reinforces the church's commitment to its mission. Celebrations also provide opportunities for members to give thanks to God and one another for their contributions and faithfulness.

Mobilizing the Church for Action

Revival in the church must lead to action. A revived church is one that is actively engaged in evangelism, discipleship, and social engagement. Mobilizing the church for action involves equipping and empowering members to live out their faith and fulfill the Great Commission.

Evangelism and Outreach Efforts

Evangelism and outreach are essential components of a revived church. A church that is experiencing revival will have a renewed passion for sharing the gospel and reaching the lost.

Training and Equipping for Evangelism: Effective evangelism requires training and equipping. Church leaders should provide resources and training to help members share their faith confidently and effectively. This includes teaching the gospel message, personal evangelism strategies, and how to engage in spiritual conversations. Training sessions, workshops, and evangelism courses can help equip members for this vital ministry.

Organizing Outreach Events: Organizing outreach events provides opportunities for the church to engage with the community and share the gospel. These events can include evangelistic crusades, community service projects, neighborhood block parties, and special worship services. Outreach events should be designed to meet the needs of the community, build relationships, and create opportunities for gospel conversations.

Encouraging Personal Evangelism: While organized outreach events are important, personal evangelism is equally crucial. Members should be encouraged to share their faith in their everyday lives, whether at work, school, or in their neighborhoods. Testimonies of personal evangelism experiences can inspire and motivate others to step out in faith and share the gospel.

Utilizing Technology and Media: In today's digital age, technology and media offer powerful tools for evangelism and outreach. Churches can use social media, websites, podcasts, and online videos to share the gospel and connect with people. Online evangelism campaigns, live-streamed services, and virtual Bible studies can reach individuals who may not attend a physical church service. I must add one note here: Technology should serve the message. It should convey the message, it shouldn't *be* the message. Technology and media can be a gimmick. Success with technology should be measured in one thing: its effectiveness at producing disciples.

Building Relationships with the Community: Building relationships with the community is essential for effective outreach. Churches should seek to understand the needs and concerns of their community and find ways to serve and build bridges. This can include partnering with local organizations, participating in community events, and offering practical assistance such as food drives, tutoring programs, and support groups. Ultimately, churches should serve the communities they are in.

"But in your hearts revere Christ as Lord. Always be prepared to give an answer to everyone who asks you to give the reason for the hope that you have. But do this with gentleness and respect, keeping a clear conscience, so that those who speak maliciously against your good behavior in Christ may be ashamed of their slander." I Peter 3:15-16

Discipleship and Mentorship Programs

Discipleship is the process of growing in faith and becoming more like Christ. A revived church prioritizes discipleship and creates opportunities for members to grow spiritually and mature in their faith. Remember, Matthew 28:19 tells us to make disciples, not converts.

Developing Discipleship Pathways: Developing clear discipleship pathways helps members understand the steps they can take to grow in their faith. This can include new believer classes, Bible study groups, discipleship courses, and mentoring relationships. Discipleship pathways should be designed to meet individuals where they are in their spiritual journey and help them progress toward spiritual maturity. Discipleship should be a well-thought-out process, not a shotgun approach. There should be a trajectory from "new Christian" to "mature Christian".

Offering Small Groups and Bible Studies: Small groups and Bible studies provide a context for in-depth study of Scripture, mutual support, and spiritual growth. These groups can focus on specific topics or books of the Bible and provide opportunities for members to ask questions, share insights, and apply biblical principles to their lives. Small groups also foster community and accountability, which are essential for discipleship.

Mentoring and One-on-One Discipleship: Mentoring relationships and one-on-one discipleship provide personalized support and guidance for spiritual growth. Mature believers can mentor newer believers, helping them navigate their spiritual journey, overcome challenges, and grow in their faith. Mentoring relationships should be characterized by mutual respect, trust, and a commitment to each other's spiritual growth. Both this and the previous paragraph fall under the truth of Proverbs 27:17, "As iron sharpens iron, so one man sharpens another."

Providing Resources and Tools for Spiritual Growth: Providing resources and tools for spiritual growth helps members develop their personal spiritual disciplines. This can include devotional books, Bible reading plans, prayer journals, and online resources. Church leaders should regularly recommend and provide access to these resources to support members in their spiritual growth.

Encouraging a Lifestyle of Discipleship: Discipleship is not just a program but a lifestyle. Church leaders should encourage members to integrate their faith into every aspect of their lives. This includes practicing spiritual disciplines, serving others, sharing their faith, and living out biblical principles in their daily lives. A lifestyle of discipleship is characterized by a continuous pursuit of spiritual growth and a commitment to following Jesus. Remember that Romans 12 tells us that we are to offer our bodies as living sacrifices, for *that* is our spiritual act of worship. What we *do* is our worship, even more so than standing in a dark room singing worship songs.

Social and Community Engagement

A revived church is actively engaged in its community, seeking to meet practical needs and demonstrate the love of Christ. Social and community engagement are tangible expressions of the church's mission and powerful witnesses to the gospel. We are called to be servants. We must move beyond the four walls of the church! We are called to put our needs behind the needs of others (Philippians 2).

Identifying Community Needs: Identifying the needs of the community is the first step in social engagement. Church leaders should seek to understand the specific challenges and opportunities in their community and find ways to address them. This can involve conducting surveys, partnering with local organizations, and building relationships with community leaders. We must understand that different communities will have different needs.

Offering Practical Assistance: Offering practical assistance demonstrates the love of Christ in tangible ways. This can include providing food and clothing, offering financial assistance, organizing job training programs, and supporting families in crisis. Practical assistance should be provided with compassion, respect, and a commitment to empowering individuals and communities. I John 3:17 says, "If anyone has material possessions and sees a brother or sister in need but has no pity on them, how can the love of God be in that person?" When I was a pastor, I made an agreement with a local grocery store—not a chain—to give any person down on their luck who I sent to the grocery store, $100 worth of groceries. We would then settle up at the end of the month and pay for the groceries that we had given to the people in need.

Advocating for Justice and Compassion: Advocacy for justice and compassion is an essential aspect of social engagement. The church should speak out against injustice, support marginalized and vulnerable populations, and work to create a more just and compassionate society. This can involve participating in advocacy campaigns, supporting social justice initiatives, and educating the congregation on issues of justice and compassion. Now, I suppose many of you are bristling at this a bit, not because the Bible clearly teaches it but because of how modern secular society has twisted that verse and the meaning behind it to include the idea that somehow we are to support and approve of sin. This is not what I am speaking of here.

Building Partnerships with Local Organizations: Building partnerships with local organizations enhances the church's ability to engage with the community effectively. Churches can collaborate with nonprofits, schools, government agencies, and other faith-based organizations to address community needs and work toward common goals. Partnerships can amplify the church's impact and provide opportunities for members to serve in various capacities.

Integrating Social Engagement into the Church's Mission: Integrating social engagement into the church's mission ensures that it is not an optional add-on but a core aspect of the church's identity and purpose. Social engagement should be woven into the fabric of the church's ministries, worship, and outreach efforts. This integration helps to create a holistic approach to ministry that reflects the heart of God for justice, compassion, and transformation.

Revival in the church involves a comprehensive renewal that touches every aspect of congregational life. Revitalizing the local church requires a commitment to prayer, repentance, and the faithful preaching of God's Word. Leadership plays a crucial role in fostering and sustaining revival by modeling spiritual disciplines, maintaining vision, and equipping others for ministry. Unity and community are essential for creating an environment where the Holy Spirit can move freely and powerfully.

Mobilizing the church for action involves engaging in evangelism and outreach, developing discipleship and mentorship programs, and actively participating in social and community engagement. A revived church is characterized by a passionate commitment to the Great Commission, a deep love for God and one another, and a desire to impact the world for Christ.

As we seek revival in our churches, let us pray fervently, repent sincerely, and commit ourselves to the mission of the gospel. May God, in His grace and mercy, pour out His Spirit upon us, renew our hearts, and transform our churches for His glory and the advancement of His Kingdom.

Chapter Four
Revival in the Family

In the pursuit of revival—both personal and societal—the family unit occupies a foundational role. Rooted in biblical principles and God's design, the family serves as the bedrock of society, shaping individuals, communities, and generations. Our family of origin is where we are supposed to learn to love, forgive, accept others, and be part of a family unit. However, in today's world marked by shifting cultural norms, societal pressures, and moral decline, the institution of the family faces challenges we have never encountered before. Yet, within these challenges lies an opportunity for revival—a spiritual awakening that restores God's intended purpose for families, strengthens marriages, nurtures children in the fear of the Lord, and impacts society for generations to come.

Restoring Family Values

At the heart of revival in the family lies the restoration of biblical values—values rooted in God's Word and His design for relationships within the family. From the very beginning, God ordained the family as the foundational unit of society, established by the covenant of marriage between one man and one woman (Genesis 2:24). Biblical principles provide a framework for family life that encompasses love, mutual respect, sacrificial service, and spiritual growth. The family is the smallest yet most powerful social group that humans have.

Biblical Principles for Family Life

The Bible provides timeless principles that guide the conduct and relationships within the family. When families experience revival, their entire lives can be changed, and they can experience life as God intends. These changes include:

Love and Respect: Ephesians 5:25 calls husbands to love their wives sacrificially, just as Christ loved the Church, and wives to respect and submit to their husbands in a loving and honoring manner. This mutual love and respect create a harmonious atmosphere where each member of the family feels valued and affirmed. The world, with the onslaught of feminism, has swayed our culture to reject Biblical values of the family and most of our families are not running according to Biblical principles.

Unity and Oneness: Jesus emphasized the unity and oneness of marriage, stating, "Therefore what God has joined together, let no one separate" (Mark 10:9). This unity extends to the entire family unit, fostering a sense of belonging, security, and mutual support. One of the great tragedies of modern American life is the break-up of so many marriages. Even Christians are not immune to divorce. Revival in the lives of couples can save marriages that are on the brink.

Training in God's Word: Deuteronomy 6:6-7 exhorts parents to diligently teach God's commandments to their children, impressing them on their hearts and minds. This biblical instruction forms the foundation of spiritual growth and moral guidance within the family.

Stewardship and Provision: The Scriptures emphasize the importance of providing for one's family (1 Timothy 5:8) and stewarding resources wisely. This includes financial stewardship, time management, and cultivating a home environment that honors God. Jesus talked a lot about money, and children can learn lessons in a Christian home that can provide benefits for a lifetime.

Addressing Challenges Facing Families Today

Revival gives strength and power to overcome trouble in families. Today's families confront a myriad of challenges that threaten them, including:

Breakdown of Marriage: High divorce rates and the redefinition of marriage pose significant challenges to family stability and the well-being of children. People are always hurt through divorce. Hearts and lives are torn apart and even if the people make it afterward, there is still damage that has to be dealt with for the rest of their lives.

Parental Absence: Due to work demands or other factors, some children experience the absence of one or both parents, impacting their emotional and spiritual development. I would say that the number one problem in American families today is the absence of one of the parents. God designed the family to have a mother and a father, bringing their unique qualities and strengths to help grow healthy and holy children. When one is absent, the family is out of balance.

Cultural Influences: Secular ideologies and cultural trends often contradict biblical values, leading to confusion and moral relativism within families. Some leaders of aberrant groups have literally said they are "coming for your children." The home is a place to protect and shield our children until they are mature enough to handle what the world throws at them. We should not keep our children from everything but only allow them to be aware when they are appropriately equipped to handle what the world throws their way.

Technology and Media: The pervasive influence of digital media and technology can undermine family relationships, distract from meaningful interactions, and expose children to harmful content. When my children were growing up, we had "no screen Sundays," which meant no TV, no computer, no phone, etc. It was a weekly break from technology and media, and I believe it was good for them, especially considering what great readers my children became.

Revival in the family addresses these challenges by reaffirming biblical principles, fostering open communication, and nurturing an environment where God's truth and love prevail. As parents, we need to be praying each and every day for our children and grandchildren, that they would come to Jesus, surrender their lives to Him, and walk with Him throughout their lives.

Role of Parents in Spiritual Leadership

Parents play a pivotal role in shaping the spiritual and moral foundations of their children. As primary influencers and role models, parents are entrusted with the responsibility to nurture their children's faith, provide godly guidance, and model a Christ-centered life. Unfortunately, many parents have abdicated the spiritual training of their children to the Church. Or even worse, they tell others that they are going to "let the kids figure out what faith they want to be." Instead, this is what godly parents should be doing:

Spiritual Instruction: Proverbs 22:6 instructs parents to "train up a child in the way he should go, and when he is old he will not depart from it." This training involves teaching children the Scriptures, praying together as a family, and imparting biblical wisdom for daily living. There are daily devotionals designed for Christian families. Each day is one page. Our children loved doing the daily devotional together as a family.

Modeling Authentic Faith: Parents are called to model authentic faith through their words and actions. Children learn about God's love, grace, and truth through observing how their parents live out their faith in practical ways. The last thing you want is for your children to say those dreaded words, "Why should I? You don't." If your faith isn't real, your children's won't be either. If you don't take Jesus seriously, neither will your children.

Discipline and Correction: Discipline, rooted in love and consistency, helps children understand the consequences of their actions and guides them toward obedience and godliness (Proverbs 13:24, Hebrews 12:6). Truly, one of the things modern parents do that demonstrates actual hatred of their children is to not discipline them and let them run wild. Children need Biblical discipline. "Chris, that is an extreme statement! Hate our children?" Well, yes. Don't argue with me. Argue with God: "Whoever spares the rod hates their children, but the one who loves their children is careful to discipline them." (Proverbs 13:24)

Cultivating a Home Environment of Love and Grace: Ephesians 6:4 charges fathers to bring up their children "in the discipline and instruction of the Lord." This instruction is to be marked by love, grace, and patience, creating a home environment where children feel safe, valued, and encouraged to grow in their faith.

Strengthening Marriages and Parenting

Strong marriages serve as the foundation for a thriving family unit and contribute to societal stability and well-being. Revival in marriages involves cultivating a relationship centered on Christ, prioritizing mutual love and respect, and navigating challenges with faith and unity.

Importance of Strong Marriages in Society: Marriage is a sacred covenant ordained by God, designed to reflect the love and unity between Christ and His Church (Ephesians 5:31-32). Strong marriages provide a stable environment for children to flourish in, promote emotional and spiritual intimacy, and serve as a testimony of God's faithfulness to the world. We need to, as wives and husbands, as mothers and fathers, dedicate ourselves to having strong and godly marriages. We should be spending time together each and every day, growing in the Lord. Every morning, Denise and I get up, make a cup of coffee, and do devotions and pray together. We can do this in about twenty minutes, and it is an incredible start to our day. We start by reading a chapter in the Bible, then a few pages in a Christian book or daily devotional. After that, we take a few minutes and pray together for our relationship, our family, and our work that day. We also pray for issues that may be going on in the world. These twenty minutes are the bedrock of our relationship.

Strategies for Godly Parenting

Prayer and Dependence on God: Recognizing their dependence on God, parents commit their children's lives and upbringing to Him in prayer, seeking His wisdom and guidance at every stage of parenting. Parents should be praying for their children's spiritual eyes and ears to be open and for them to have the spiritual armor they need to stand against the devil's schemes (Ephesians 6).

Biblical Teaching and Discipleship: Intentional teaching of Scripture and discipleship within the home equips children with a biblical worldview and prepares them to face life's challenges with faith and resilience. This can be done one-on-one, during family devotions, and through having them involved in a Biblically based youth group. Better yet, all three combined.

Setting Godly Examples: Parents model godly character, integrity, and compassion, demonstrating Christ-like virtues in their interactions with each other and their children. First, we set expectations with our children so they know what to do. Secondly, and this is the power behind setting expectations, we must model that behavior! If we don't do what we tell them to do, their opinion of us will be that we are hypocrites.

Open Communication and Listening: Creating a culture of open communication allows children to express their thoughts, questions, and concerns, fostering trust and understanding within the family. We must be willing to hear from our children. They must know that we care. And the older they get, the more we must treat them age appropriately. For example, with my grown children—the youngest is twenty-one—I don't just give them advice. Most of the time I start with, "Would you like my take?"

Revival in the family is not merely a personal or private matter; it is a societal imperative and a spiritual necessity. By restoring biblical values, nurturing strong marriages, and equipping parents for godly parenting, families become agents of God's Kingdom and bearers of His light in a darkened world. As Christians embrace their roles as spiritual leaders within their homes, they contribute to a broader movement of revival that impacts communities, cultures, and nations. I hope that this chapter inspires and equips families to pursue revival wholeheartedly, trusting in God's transforming power to heal, strengthen, and restore families for His glory and the advancement of His Kingdom.

Chapter Five
Revival in Education

Education, as a cornerstone of societal development, plays a pivotal role in shaping minds, values, and the future of nations. From a biblical perspective, the pursuit of revival in education entails recognizing the historical impact of Christianity, addressing contemporary challenges, and seizing opportunities to impart a biblical worldview and spiritual renewal within schools and universities.

Christian Influence in Education—The Battle for Biblical Values in American Education

From a biblical perspective, the landscape of American education today—encompassing schools, colleges, and universities—presents a battlefield where traditional biblical values are increasingly under siege. This conflict is not merely a matter of differing opinions but a profound ideological clash that strikes at the heart of moral and spiritual principles foundational to the Christian faith. We are in an epic and world-changing conflict between two worldviews: The one that says God is real and truth is real and the other that says that there is no God, truth is not absolute, and the State controls our children. Diabolical forces set out in the 1960s to take over our educational system, and they have. It is time for us to take it back.

Erosion of Moral Absolutes

One of the most conspicuous battlegrounds is the erosion of moral absolutes. Traditional biblical values uphold absolute truths, including the sanctity of life, the definition of marriage as a union between one man and one woman, and the inherent value of each individual created in the image of God. And could you imagine what our ancestors, who gave their lives for our country, would say about the mutilation of a young woman's breasts being cut off in her early teens because she "feels like a boy?" We have lost touch with the truth and many live under the lawlessness and delusion mentioned in II Thessalonians 2:10-12: "And with all the deception of wickedness for those who perish, because they did not accept the love of the truth so as to be saved. For this reason, God will send upon them a deluding influence so that they will believe what is false, in order that they all may be judged who did not believe the truth, but took pleasure in wickedness."

Contemporary educational institutions promote relativism, where moral and ethical standards are seen as fluid and subjective. This shift undermines the biblical worldview that grounds moral behavior in the unchanging nature of God. For instance, issues such as abortion and same-sex marriage are frequently discussed within educational settings without acknowledging the biblical stance. Pro-life perspectives, rooted in the belief that life begins at conception and is sacred, are often marginalized or dismissed. Similarly, the biblical view of marriage is increasingly portrayed as outdated or intolerant, replaced by a more inclusive but biblically incongruent understanding of marriage and sexuality. Parents must, if they send their children to government schools, be as involved as possible, especially in getting involved with school boards who determine what will be taught to the children in their area.

Secularization of Education

The secularization of education is another front in this ideological war. Historically, many of America's earliest colleges and universities were founded on Christian principles. Today, however, secularism dominates, pushing faith and spirituality to the margins. Prayer, Bible reading, and open discussion of Christian beliefs are often restricted or outright banned in public schools, creating an environment where students are subtly taught that faith is irrelevant to public life and intellectual pursuits.

In higher education, this secular trend is even more pronounced. Many universities promote a worldview that excludes God and dismisses religious faith as unscientific or irrational. Courses and curricula often prioritize humanistic and materialistic perspectives, fostering an academic atmosphere where faith is seen as a private matter, detached from the pursuit of knowledge and truth.

We must pray for revival on our college campuses. The evil one is powerful, but God is all-powerful. If His Spirit sweeps through a college campus, nothing can stop it.

Intellectual Hostility to Faith

Intellectual hostility towards faith further intensifies this conflict. Christian students and faculty in secular institutions frequently encounter skepticism and even open hostility towards their beliefs. This can manifest in various forms, from the ridicule of creationist views in science classes to the marginalization of Christian ethics in discussions on social and political issues. Such an environment can be intimidating for believers, who may feel pressured to conform to secular norms or remain silent about their faith.

Furthermore, the promotion of ideologies such as critical race theory and postmodernism within academic circles challenges the biblical understanding of truth, justice, and human identity. These ideologies often encourage viewing society through the lenses of power dynamics and oppression, promoting a narrative that can conflict with the Christian message of redemption, reconciliation, and the inherent worth of every person.

Hope and Response

Despite these challenges, there is hope for those committed to upholding biblical values. Believers can use several strategies to navigate and counteract the secular tide in education. First, strengthening Christian education; homeschooling and private Christian schools and colleges offer a way to provide students with an education rooted in biblical truth. Second, supporting Christian clubs, organizations, and campus ministries can create communities where students can grow in their faith and witness to their peers.

Additionally, Christians in the educational sector—whether teachers, administrators, or students—are called to be salt and light, exemplifying Christ-like love, integrity, and wisdom. By respectfully and thoughtfully engaging with opposing viewpoints, they can bear witness to the truth of the gospel in a way that is compelling and transformative. I heard someone suggest that until the secular schools are brought back to at least being neutral toward faith, Christian children should not attend, but Christian teachers should absolutely go into careers in government schools. Our children are then protected, and the other children have access to Christians who can be an influence in their lives.

The battle for traditional biblical values in American education is a significant and ongoing challenge. However, through prayer, education, and active engagement, Christians can stand firm in their faith and work towards a future where biblical principles are once again respected and upheld in the public square.

Historical Role of Christianity in American Education

Christianity has historically played a foundational role in shaping the educational landscape of America. Early educational institutions such as Harvard, Princeton, and Yale were founded with a Christian mission to educate leaders who would serve society with both intellectual rigor and moral integrity. The integration of biblical teachings and values into education was seen as essential for nurturing well-rounded individuals capable of contributing positively to their communities.

In fact, several Ivy League schools were originally founded as Christian institutions or seminaries. Here's a list of those schools along with a brief history of their Christian origins:

Harvard University (Founded in 1636): Established by the Massachusetts Bay Colony, Harvard was initially created to train clergy for the Puritan church. The school's original mission was to ensure that the future leaders of the colony would be well-versed in Christian theology and scripture.

Yale University (Founded in 1701): Yale was founded by Congregationalist ministers seeking to establish an institution to educate clergy in Connecticut. It was initially known as the Collegiate School.

Princeton University (Founded in 1746): Originally known as the College of New Jersey, Princeton was founded by New Light Presbyterians to train ministers following the Great Awakening, a series of religious revivals in the American colonies.

Columbia University (Founded in 1754): Columbia, originally named King's College, was founded by the Church of England (Anglican Church) to provide education for church members and the community.

Brown University (Founded in 1764): Brown was established by Baptists to provide education to clergy and laypeople alike, with a commitment to religious freedom and the inclusion of students from all denominations.

Dartmouth College (Founded in 1769): Dartmouth was founded by Eleazar Wheelock, a Congregational minister, with the initial purpose of educating Native Americans and training Congregationalist ministers.

These universities have since evolved into secular institutions, but their origins are deeply rooted in Christian education and theology.

Challenges Facing Christian Education Today

Despite its historical significance, Christian education faces numerous challenges in the contemporary educational landscape:

Secularization: Increasing secularization has marginalized the influence of Christian values in public schools and universities, creating tensions over issues such as religious freedom, curriculum content, and moral education. Unfortunately, uninformed Christians have allowed their schools to be taken over by people who immediately drove them out.

Worldview Conflicts: The clash between biblical worldview and secular ideologies poses challenges for Christian educators in maintaining fidelity to their faith while navigating diverse cultural perspectives.

Educational Standards: Striking a balance between academic excellence and biblical principles requires Christian schools and universities to uphold rigorous educational standards while integrating faith-based teachings.

Cultural Opposition: Christian educators may face cultural opposition and legal challenges related to issues such as gender identity, sexuality education, and religious expression in educational settings.

Opportunities for Revival in Schools and Universities—Embracing a Biblical Worldview in Education

A biblical worldview provides a comprehensive framework for understanding God's truth and His purposes for humanity. It emphasizes the integration of faith and learning across disciplines, equipping students to critically engage with academic subjects through the lens of Scripture:

Integration of Faith and Learning: Christian educators strive to integrate biblical principles into every aspect of the curriculum, from history and science to literature and ethics. This holistic approach fosters intellectual growth while nurturing spiritual maturity among students.

Cultural Engagement: Engaging with contemporary issues from a biblical perspective equips students to address cultural challenges with wisdom, compassion, and a commitment to truth.

Critical Thinking and Discernment: By cultivating critical thinking skills rooted in Scripture, Christian education empowers students to discern truth from falsehood and to defend their faith in an increasingly secularized society.

Role of Christian Educators and Institutions

Christian educators serve as mentors, role models, and spiritual guides for students, embodying Christ-like virtues and imparting values that transcend academic knowledge. We should do all we can to train Christian educators who can go into secular schools as salt and light. Doing so allows them to be involved in the following:

Discipleship and Mentorship: Beyond academic instruction, Christian educators prioritize discipleship and mentorship, nurturing students' spiritual growth and character development.

Prayer and Spiritual Formation: Intentional prayer and spiritual formation programs create opportunities for students to encounter God's presence, deepen their faith, and discern His calling for their lives.

Community and Fellowship: Establishing a supportive community of faith within educational institutions fosters unity, accountability, and mutual encouragement among students, faculty, and staff.

Stories of Revival in Educational Settings

Throughout history and in contemporary times, stories of revival in educational settings testify to God's transformative power and the impact of Christian influence:

Here are some notable examples of Christian revivals that began on college campuses in the last 100 years:

Asbury College Revival (1970):
Location: Asbury College (now Asbury University), Wilmore, Kentucky.

Description: On February 3, 1970, a regular chapel service turned into a spontaneous revival meeting that lasted for 144 hours. The revival saw continuous prayer, testimonies, and worship, drawing students, faculty, and visitors. It had a lasting impact on the campus and led to similar revivals at other colleges and universities.

Wheaton College Revival (1995):
Location: Wheaton College, Wheaton, Illinois.

Description: In March 1995, during a scheduled chapel service, students began to confess sins and seek spiritual renewal. The service extended for several days, characterized by repentance, worship, and testimonies. The revival spread to other campuses and influenced the broader evangelical community.

Howard Payne University Revival (1995):
Location: Howard Payne University, Brownwood, Texas.

Description: A significant revival occurred at Howard Payne University in January 1995, beginning with a student-led prayer meeting. The revival included extended times of worship, confession, and prayer, and it impacted other nearby campuses.

Samford University Revival (2010):
Location: Samford University, Birmingham, Alabama.

Description: In 2010, a spontaneous revival broke out during a student-led worship service. It led to several days of continuous worship, prayer, and repentance, significantly impacting the student body and faculty.

Most recently, in 2023, we saw mini revivals break out at a number of colleges that made the news for their revivals. Revivals broke out at Asbury, Lee University, Western Kentucky, Cedarville University, Texas A&M Corpus Christi, and Auburn, among others. There were also reports of revival breaking out across the HBCUs (Historically Black Colleges and Universities) through a group called the Black Voices Movement. All of this is very encouraging to those who worry about our future generations. These revivals illustrate the ongoing potential for spiritual renewal on college campuses, often characterized by spontaneous prayer, confession, worship, and a deep sense of God's presence among students.

Ultimately revival in education is a call to reclaim the foundational principles of Christian influence and spiritual renewal within schools and universities. By embracing a biblical worldview, addressing contemporary challenges with faith and wisdom, and equipping the next generation of leaders with both intellectual rigor and spiritual depth, Christian educators and institutions play a crucial role in shaping the future of society. As we reflect on the historical impact of Christianity in education, confront present-day challenges, and celebrate stories of revival, may we remain steadfast in our commitment to uphold God's truth, advance His Kingdom, and empower students to impact the world for His glory and the flourishing of humanity.

Chapter Six
Revival in the Marketplace

In the realm of business and commerce, the concept of revival extends beyond traditional religious settings to encompass a transformational movement where faith intersects with work, ethics align with values, and businesses become agents of societal good. From a biblical perspective, revival in the marketplace involves integrating faith principles, empowering Christian leaders, addressing ethical challenges, and envisioning industries transformed by God's principles of justice, integrity, and compassion.

Integrating Faith and Work

When I was a church pastor, I regularly reminded my congregation that because of the secularization of our country, they had far more ability to speak to modern people about God than I did. A hundred years ago, pastors were respected, even if the other person didn't agree with their Christian faith. Now, pastors are dismissed and avoided. They no longer hold the esteem they once had, and their voices are less impactful in modern culture. But Christian businesspeople, active in their workplace, have tremendous opportunities to make a significant impact in the marketplace.

The integration of faith and work is foundational to experiencing revival in the marketplace. It entails recognizing that work is a calling from God—an opportunity to glorify Him through ethical conduct, excellence, and service. Work *is* ministry!

Biblical Foundation: Colossians 3:23-24 instructs, "Whatever you do, do your work heartily, as for the Lord and not for people...It is the Lord

Christ whom you serve." This biblical perspective shifts the focus from self-interest to stewardship and service, elevating the purpose of work beyond financial gain, to honoring God and serving others. Work isn't just a place you go to earn money. It is a place to live out your faith and minister to those who you interact with each and every day.

Ethical Standards: Integrating faith into business practices involves upholding ethical standards rooted in Scripture, such as honesty, fairness, respect for human dignity, and environmental stewardship. Unfortunately, many Christians do not live out their Sunday morning faith when they are at work. All too many Christian businesspeople have given the rest of us bad reputations because people see them say they believe one thing and then do another. I once had a best-selling author with over thirty million copies in print, who is not a Christian, tell me that if anyone she is thinking about getting into business with announces they are a Christian during the negotiations to work together, she pulls the plug on the deal. Frankly, she said, she had just been burned by too many Christians. I told her that I am a Christian and that I would never lie to her. She told me that she knew that and that was the only reason she took the meeting. How sad though, that we Christians are keeping people from Christ with unethical business practices.

Witness and Mission: The workplace becomes a platform for Christian witness and mission, where believers demonstrate Christ-like values through their actions, decisions, and interactions with colleagues, clients, and stakeholders. We must remember that we are ambassadors of Christ to the world we live in, including our workplaces.

Role of Christian Business Leaders

Christian business leaders play a crucial role in advancing revival in the marketplace by embodying Christ-centered leadership principles and fostering environments where faith flourishes. Three things in particular come to mind.

Servant Leadership: Following Jesus' example of servant leadership (Mark 10:45), Christian leaders prioritize humility, compassion, and selflessness in their relationships and decision-making. I was fortunate in my mid-thirties to co-host a television show with the legendary motivational speaker, Zig Ziglar, who was a devout Christian. One of Zig's most famous quotes is "You can have everything in life you want if you will just help other people get what they want." This is a great way of reminding us that we are first and foremost to be servants of those around us. I like the reminder from Philippians 2:3-4:

"Do nothing from selfishness or empty conceit, but with humility consider one another as more important than yourselves; do not merely look out for your own personal interests, but also for the interests of others."

Integrity and Transparency: Upholding integrity and transparency builds trust and credibility, reflecting God's character of truthfulness and reliability (Proverbs 11:3, Ephesians 4:25). As Christians in the marketplace, we must operate out of a single set of morals, ethics, and values—not multiple. We must base everything on the teachings of scripture. They must be foundational. We can't have Biblical values on Sunday morning and Wednesday night and then abandon them the rest of the week.

Discipleship and Mentorship: Investing in the spiritual and professional development of employees fosters a culture of growth, equipping individuals to integrate faith into their work and daily lives. The workplace is an excellent place to mentor others. Of course, legalities and pressure from secularists who want faith removed from all public areas can make this a challenge, but it can be done. Pray for opportunities to minister to others.

Ethical Challenges in the Marketplace

The marketplace presents numerous ethical challenges that require discernment, courage, and adherence to biblical principles. Staying close to the Lord is imperative to withstand the temptations that can come in the workplace. Here are just a few:

Corruption and Bribery: The temptation to compromise ethical standards for personal gain or competitive advantage undermines trust and integrity within business transactions. There are many warnings against bribery in the scriptures, most notably in the book of Proverbs.

"He who profits illicitly troubles his own house, but he who hates bribes will live." Proverbs 15:27 (NASB)

"A bribe is a charm in the sight of its owner; wherever he turns, he prospers." Proverbs 17:8 (NASB)

"To show partiality is not good, because for a piece of bread, a man will do wrong." Proverbs 28:21 (NIV)

These proverbs highlight the moral and ethical implications of bribery, as well as its potential to corrupt integrity.

Labor Practices: Ensuring fair wages, safe working conditions, and respect for human rights aligns with biblical mandates to treat employees justly and compassionately (James 5:4).

Environmental Responsibility: Stewardship of natural resources and environmental sustainability reflects God's call to care for creation (Genesis 2:15), requiring businesses to adopt practices that minimize ecological impact.

Opportunities for Witness and Impact

Amidst ethical challenges, the marketplace also offers unique opportunities for Christian witness and societal impact on a daily basis if we open our eyes to the opportunity. We must be purposeful when we go to work, asking God to open doors to people we can serve and influence for the Kingdom.

Customer Relations: Building relationships based on trust, respect, and genuine care for customers provides opportunities to share the love of Christ through acts of service and integrity. The way you handle yourself is being watched closely. We do not want to bring disrepute to the Lord with bad behavior.

The Way We Treat Our Employees: While the Bible doesn't explicitly talk about how to treat employees, there are passages where the principles fit accordingly.

"And masters, do the same things to them, and give up threatening, knowing that both their Master and yours is in Heaven, and there is no partiality with Him." Ephesians 6:9 (NASB)

"Masters, grant your slaves justice and fairness, knowing that you also have a Master in Heaven." Colossians 4:1 (NASB)

"Behold, the pay of the laborers who mowed your fields, and which has been withheld by you, cries out against you; and the outcry of those who did the harvesting has reached the ears of the Lord of armies." James 5:4 (NASB)

These passages collectively underscore the principles of fairness, respect, and accountability that should guide Christian employers in their relationships with their employees.

Philanthropy and Community Engagement: Investing in community development, charitable initiatives, and social justice initiatives demonstrates Christ's compassion for the marginalized and vulnerable (Matthew 25:35-40).

Transforming Industries—The Impact of Revival on Various Sectors

Revival in the marketplace has the potential to transform industries by infusing them with biblical values, ethical standards, and a commitment to societal welfare.

Healthcare: Christian healthcare providers integrate faith into patient care, promoting holistic healing and compassionate service rooted in Christ's love and compassion. Healthcare under biblical guidelines would also preclude what many are calling "gender-affirming care," when it is really child mutilation. Health-sharing organizations, many of which are run by and for Christians, can save people hundreds if not thousands of dollars a month and provide them with better health care.

Technology: Ethical considerations in technology development prioritize privacy, data security, and ethical artificial intelligence, aligning with biblical principles of justice and respect for human dignity. Technology has the potential for both great good and great evil. Christians in tech can be a force for good.

Finance and Economics: Applying biblical principles of stewardship and financial integrity fosters economic sustainability, fairness in financial transactions, and support for those in need (Luke 6:38). Understanding and promoting Biblical financial principles can help people have a better life and feel more secure.

Case Studies of Businesses Influenced by Christian Principles

Numerous businesses and organizations exemplify the transformative impact of Christian principles in the marketplace, showing that you can serve God and be successful financially:

Chick-fil-A: Known for its commitment to closing on Sundays to honor the Sabbath and treating employees with respect and care, reflecting Christian values in business operations.

Hobby Lobby: Fought for religious freedom in front of the Supreme Court and adopted the Bible as a guide for business, promoting ethical standards and moral values in all aspects of operations.

Interstate Batteries: Interstate Batteries is known for its commitment to Christian values, which are reflected in its mission statement and business practices. The company emphasizes integrity, respect, and servant leadership, and CEO Norm Miller is vocal about his Christian faith.

Tyson Foods: Tyson Foods, one of the world's largest food companies, was founded by John W. Tyson, who instilled Christian principles in the company's culture. The company has a chaplaincy program to support employees and promotes values such as faith, family, and hard work.

ServiceMaster: ServiceMaster, the parent company of brands like Merry Maids and Terminix, was founded by Marion E. Wade, who incorporated Christian principles into the company's operations. The company's mission includes honoring God in all they do and helping people develop.

Alaska Airlines: Alaska Airlines has a history of incorporating Christian values into its company culture. It is known for treating employees and customers with respect and kindness, and for its practice of including prayer cards on meal trays until 2012.

Forever 21: Forever 21, a popular clothing retailer, is known for its founders' Christian faith. The company includes Bible verses on the bottom of its shopping bags and is committed to ethical business practices influenced by their beliefs.

While these companies are certainly not perfect, we should thank God for these companies and their leaders who show that the tenets of Christianity can be successful as business principles.

Vision for a Marketplace Transformed by Revival

A marketplace transformed by revival is characterized by:

Cultural Renewal: Infusing societal norms with biblical values, such as justice, compassion, honesty, and integrity, leads to cultural renewal and societal transformation.

Kingdom Impact: Advancing God's Kingdom by leveraging business influence to promote spiritual renewal, social justice, and the proclamation of the gospel.

Global Witness: Extending Christian witness and humanitarian aid globally, demonstrating Christ's love through international business partnerships and missions.

Commitment to Ongoing Revival

Continued revival in the marketplace requires:

Prayer and Dependence on God: Seeking God's guidance, wisdom, and empowerment through prayer is essential for sustaining revival and overcoming challenges. Many Christians pray for their church and their families, but how many pray over their businesses? I think very few. Unfortunately, many Christians compartmentalize their faith and their business separately from one another. Our faith should be a part of *everything* we do, including our businesses. This is why we must raise our businesses before the throne of Heaven!

Collaboration and Unity: Fostering collaboration among Christian businesses, organizations, and leaders enhances collective impact and promotes unity in advancing God's Kingdom. What would happen in a town if all the Christian-owned businesses came together for their community? Something good, I am sure!

Faithful Witness: Remaining steadfast in faith, integrity, and courage, even in the face of opposition or adversity, bears witness to God's transformative power in the marketplace. We should live our business lives in such a way that people see our God as a good God!

Revival in the marketplace is not merely a theoretical concept but a practical outworking of faith and obedience in everyday business practices. By integrating faith and work, addressing ethical challenges with biblical wisdom, and envisioning industries transformed by God's principles, Christian business leaders and organizations can catalyze societal change and advance the agenda of God's Kingdom. I hope this chapter inspires and equips believers to embrace their roles as ambassadors of Christ in the marketplace, leading with integrity, humility, and a commitment to excellence, for the glory of God and the flourishing of humanity.

Chapter Seven
Revival in Government and Politics

The intersection of faith and governance holds profound implications for social justice, moral integrity, and the flourishing of nations. From a biblical perspective, revival in government and politics involves grounding leadership and policies in biblical principles, understanding historical Christian influence, navigating the contemporary political landscape, and engaging in transformative practices that uphold righteousness and justice.

Biblical Perspective on Government—The Role of Government According to Scripture

Scripture provides foundational principles for understanding the role and responsibilities of government:

Romans 13:1-7: Affirms the authority of government instituted by God to uphold justice, maintain order, and promote the common good.

Look specifically at verse one:

> "Every person is to be subject to the governing authorities. For there is no authority except from God, and those which exist are established by God."

1 Timothy 2:1-2: Instructs believers to pray for all those in authority, highlighting the importance of governance guided by God's wisdom and righteousness. In fact, it says that praying for our leaders *pleases* God. Why? Because He wants all men to be saved.

Proverbs 29:4: "The king gives stability to the land by justice, but a person who takes bribes ruins it." This verse underscores the importance of righteous leadership in ensuring societal stability and flourishing. If we want a righteous nation, we should look for a leader who is righteous. If none are to be found, we should at least look for those who are sympathetic to the Judeo-Christian worldview.

Historical Influence of Christianity on American Politics

The Founding Fathers of the United States, a group of influential leaders and visionaries, played a pivotal role in the nation's birth and development. While they were not all Christians by faith, their guiding principles, deeply embedded in Christian values, are evident in the seminal documents they created, such as the Declaration of Independence and the Constitution. The Christian principles of liberty, equality, and moral order were not only personal convictions for many of these leaders but also foundational elements that shaped the new nation's political and social landscape.

One of the most significant influences on the Founding Fathers was the Christian concept of liberty. The notion that all individuals are endowed by their Creator with inherent rights resonated deeply with these leaders. This belief is explicitly stated in the Declaration of Independence, which asserts that all men are created equal and endowed by their Creator with certain unalienable rights, among them: life, liberty, and the pursuit of happiness. This declaration reflects the Christian understanding that true liberty is a God-given right, not something granted by human governments. The Founding Fathers' commitment to this principle was a driving force behind their fight for independence from British rule and their determination to establish a government that would protect these fundamental rights.

Equality, another core Christian principle, significantly influenced the Founding Fathers. The idea that all human beings are created in the image of God and therefore possess inherent worth and dignity was revolutionary in a time when social hierarchies and class distinctions were the norms. The Founders sought to create a society where individuals were judged not by their social status or wealth but by their character and actions. This is reflected in the Constitution, which aims to establish justice and promote the general welfare, ensuring that all citizens are treated equally under the law. The commitment to equality is further exemplified by the gradual abolition of slavery, as the moral and ethical implications of inequality became increasingly indefensible for a nation founded on Christian ideals.

Moral order, a cornerstone of Christian teaching, also played a crucial role in shaping the vision of the Founding Fathers. The belief that a just and prosperous society must be grounded in moral and ethical principles is evident in their writings and actions. The Constitution's Preamble speaks to this vision, aiming to "establish justice, ensure domestic tranquility, provide for the common defense, promote the general welfare, and secure the blessings of liberty to ourselves and our posterity." These objectives are rooted in a desire to create a society governed by laws that reflect a higher moral order, one that ensures fairness, peace, and the well-being of all its citizens. In fact, President John Adams wrote in a letter dated October 11, 1798, to the Massachusetts Militia, "Our Constitution was made only for a moral and religious people. It is wholly inadequate to the government of any other."

The Founding Fathers' integration of Christian principles into the nation's founding documents has had a lasting impact on American society. Their emphasis on liberty, equality, and moral order laid the foundation for a nation that strives to uphold these values in its laws and institutions. While the United States has faced numerous challenges and struggles in living up to these ideals, including the efforts to eradicate them from American society, the guiding principles established by the Founding Fathers continue to inspire and shape the nation's pursuit of a more just and equitable society.

The Christian principles of liberty, equality, and moral order profoundly influenced the Founding Fathers and are deeply embedded in the

Declaration of Independence and the Constitution. These principles not only guided the creation of the United States but also continue to serve as a beacon for the nation's ongoing journey toward realizing the vision of a society where all individuals are free, equal, and governed by a just moral order.

Challenges in the Contemporary Political Landscape

The current political landscape presents various challenges that necessitate revival and moral renewal:

Partisanship

Partisan polarization in contemporary American politics has become a significant barrier to effective governance. As ideological and religious divisions deepen, the capacity for bipartisan cooperation and compromise—essential components for a functioning democracy—diminishes. This increasing polarization is characterized by political parties and their supporters moving further apart on the ideological and religious spectrum, leading to a more contentious and adversarial political environment.

Polarization erodes public trust in governmental institutions. As partisan rhetoric intensifies, voters often perceive the other side not merely as opponents but as existential threats to their values and way of life. This heightened animosity fuels a cycle of distrust and hostility, making it even more challenging to find common ground. The result is a fragmented society where political discourse is dominated by division rather than dialogue. This is why many today believe that America is already in a civil war—albeit a non-violent one. These aren't just disagreements we have anymore.

I believe we have come to the place where the only answer is revival. Unless those who do not hold Judeo-Christian views are converted, we will never have peace with them because they will always push for a Secular-Humanist/Marxist outcome.

Ethical Dilemmas

Ethical dilemmas such as corruption, dishonesty, and ethical compromises profoundly undermine public trust in government institutions and leaders. The Bible is unequivocal in its condemnation of corrupt practices and dishonest behavior. Proverbs 11:3 states, "The integrity of the upright will guide them, but the perversity of the treacherous will destroy them." For Christians, ethical leadership rooted in biblical principles is not just desirable but imperative for the health and well-being of society.

Corruption and dishonesty in government create a chasm between leaders and the people they serve. When leaders engage in unethical practices, they violate the trust placed in them by their constituents. This breach of trust erodes the moral foundation upon which effective governance is built. Romans 13:1-2 calls for submission to governing authorities, acknowledging that their authority comes from God. However, when those in power engage in corruption, they distort the divine mandate of their position, leading to disillusionment and cynicism among the public.

Furthermore, ethical compromises by leaders set a damaging precedent for society at large. When those in power are seen acting unethically without consequence, it can lead to a broader acceptance of unethical behavior across all levels of society. Micah 6:8 emphasizes what God requires of us: "to do justice, to love kindness, and to walk humbly with your God." Leaders are called to exemplify these virtues, serving as moral beacons for the communities they lead.

For Christians, the Bible's teachings on honesty and integrity are clear. Ephesians 4:25 urges believers to rid themselves of falsehood and speak truthfully, reflecting the expectation that truthfulness should permeate all aspects of life, including governance. When leaders fail to uphold these values, it not only damages public trust but also hinders the potential for a just and righteous society.

Ultimately, corruption, dishonesty, and ethical compromises are not just political issues but moral failings that undermine public trust in government institutions and leaders. Upholding the biblical principles of integrity, honesty, and justice is crucial for restoring faith in governance and fostering a society that reflects God's standards.

Social Justice Issues

Social justice issues like human rights, immigration reform, healthcare access, and environmental stewardship are integral to living out biblical principles. These concerns call for ethical leadership and compassionate policies firmly rooted in the concept of *Biblical* justice, which emphasizes the inherent dignity and worth of every individual as created in the image of God (Genesis 1:27). It is important to note that even among those who claim to be Christian, there are differing views of how social justice should be done and what should be included. I do believe that there is a faction of "Christians" who are using their "faith" to promote not Biblical social justice, but leftist/Marxist social justice masquerading as "Christianity." But we cannot throw out the baby with the bathwater. As you read the following, ask yourself what the Biblical command is, not what a particular person, politician, pundit, or pastor may tell you it is.

Human rights are central to the Christian faith. The Bible teaches that all people are created by God and deserve to be treated with respect and dignity. Proverbs 31:8-9 urges believers to "Open your mouth for the people who cannot speak, for the rights of all the unfortunate." This scriptural mandate calls for Christians to advocate for the oppressed and marginalized, ensuring their rights are protected and their voices heard. The church must come to grips with the fact that we have often forgotten "the least of these."

Immigration reform is another critical issue. The Bible frequently addresses the treatment of foreigners, reminding believers to welcome and care for them. Leviticus 19:34 states, "The stranger who resides with you shall be to you as the native among you, and you shall love him as yourself, for you were strangers in the land of Egypt." This command highlights the importance of compassionate and just policies that honor the dignity of immigrants. Again, there are two factions here. One side pretends to have compassion under the guise of "faith," but has no desire to uphold the law, showing they are not actually upholding Biblical values. America has always been a country that values immigration, but most importantly, *legal immigration*. True Christianity upholds immigration as long as it is *legal*. Those who promote *illegal* immigration betray themselves and show that they are not operating out of a fundamental principle of Christianity, which is to uphold the laws of a nation (Romans 13).

Access to healthcare aligns with the Biblical principle of caring for the sick and vulnerable. Jesus' ministry was marked by healing and compassion. Matthew 25:36 recounts Jesus saying, "I was sick, and you visited Me." Christians are called to support healthcare policies that provide for those in need, reflecting Christ's love and compassion. Christian revival will open hearts to compassion for the sick and vulnerable among us.

Environmental stewardship is also a biblical mandate. God entrusted humanity with the responsibility to care for His creation (Genesis 2:15). Ethical leadership must promote policies that protect and sustain the environment, ensuring that future generations can enjoy the beauty and resources of God's creation. While there is massive debate around this issue, with literally trillions of dollars on the line—meaning charlatans are circling for a piece of the pie—we must understand that we are stewards of our earth and should act accordingly.

Addressing social justice issues such as human rights, immigration reform, healthcare access, and environmental stewardship requires leaders who are guided by Biblical justice, not vogue political rhetoric. Ethical and compassionate policies that honor the dignity of every person and care for God's creation are essential for building a just and righteous society. Revival, with the millions of hearts it will turn toward Jesus, is the answer.

Engaging in the Public Square

In a time of widespread societal upheaval and moral decay, the call for revival in America is needed more than ever. This revival extends beyond the walls of the church and into the public sphere. Christian engagement in politics involves proactive participation in public discourse, advocacy for justice, and the promotion of policies aligned with biblical values. Unfortunately, many Christians today wrongly believe that they shouldn't be involved in politics. Sports, sure, but things that actually change the lives of hundreds of millions of people? Not so much. Revival brings people to understand the importance of strategic advocacy, civic responsibility, and public leadership—all grounded in Scripture.

Strategic Advocacy

Advocating for policies that promote human flourishing, protect vulnerable populations, and uphold moral principles grounded in Scripture is a crucial aspect of Christian political engagement. Proverbs 31:8-9 instructs us to "open your mouth for the people who cannot speak, for the rights of all the unfortunate." This call to action requires believers to advocate for justice and righteousness in the public arena.

Strategic advocacy means using our voices and influence to shape policies that reflect God's heart for justice and mercy. This includes promoting laws that protect the sanctity of life, defend religious freedoms, and ensure the dignity of every human being. For example, supporting policies that combat human trafficking and provide care for the homeless aligns with biblical mandates to care for the least among us (Matthew 25:40). In doing so, Christians act as God's ambassadors, reflecting His love and justice in tangible ways.

Civic Responsibility

Exercising civic responsibilities, such as voting, volunteering, and engaging in grassroots activism, is essential for influencing political outcomes and promoting the common good. Romans 13:1-7 emphasizes the importance of submitting to governing authorities and participating in the civic life of the community. By voting, Christians help elect leaders who share their values and who will enact policies that honor God.

Beyond voting, volunteering for campaigns and causes that advance biblical principles can make a significant impact. Grassroots activism, such as organizing community events, participating in peaceful protests, and engaging in local government meetings, allows believers to influence public policy and raise awareness about critical issues. Nehemiah's leadership in rebuilding Jerusalem's walls (Nehemiah 2:17-18) serves as a biblical example of civic engagement and the importance of collective action for the common good.

Civic responsibility also includes being well-informed about current events and understanding the implications of various policies. Christians are called to be discerning and wise, as stated in James 1:5, "If any of you lacks wisdom, let him ask of God, who gives to all generously and without reproach, and it will be given to him." This wisdom enables believers to navigate the complexities of the political landscape and make decisions that align with God's will.

Public Leadership

Christians called to political leadership are tasked with exemplifying servant leadership, integrity, and a commitment to advancing justice and righteousness in governance. Jesus modeled servant leadership, teaching that true leaders are those who serve others (Mark 10:42-45). Christian leaders in politics are therefore called to prioritize the welfare of their constituents and lead with humility and compassion.

Integrity is a hallmark of godly leadership. Proverbs 11:3 states, "The integrity of the upright will guide them, but the perversity of the treacherous will destroy them." Leaders who adhere to biblical values maintain honesty, transparency, and accountability in their actions. This integrity fosters trust and credibility, enabling them to effectively advocate for just and righteous policies.

Moreover, Christian leaders are called to advance justice and righteousness, reflecting God's character in their governance. Micah 6:8 outlines this divine mandate, "He has told you, mortal one, what is good; and what does the Lord require of you but to do justice, to love kindness, and to walk humbly with your God." Leaders who prioritize justice create fair and equitable laws that protect the vulnerable and promote the common good.

Revival Through Political Engagement

Revival in America requires Christians to engage in politics proactively and purposefully. This engagement involves advocating for policies that uphold biblical values, fulfilling civic responsibilities with diligence and discernment, and exemplifying godly leadership in the public sphere. As believers step into these roles, they become instruments of God's transformative power, working to bring about a society that reflects His justice, mercy, and righteousness. Unfortunately, many people do not view politics as a profession that is honorable. We need to change that perspective!

The vision for a revived America is one where biblical principles guide public policy, where leaders are characterized by integrity and servant leadership, and where citizens are actively involved in shaping a just and compassionate society. Such a revival not only addresses the moral and ethical dilemmas of our time but also paves the way for a nation that honors God in all its endeavors.

Christian engagement in politics is a vital component of revival in America. Through strategic advocacy, civic responsibility, and public leadership, believers can influence the political landscape in ways that align with biblical values and principles. As we faithfully answer this call, we contribute to the revival and renewal of our nation, advancing God's Kingdom and His purposes on earth.

Importance of Prayer for National Leaders—Biblical Mandate for Prayer

1 Timothy 2:1-2 states, "First of all, then, I urge that requests, prayers, intercession, and thanksgiving be made on behalf of all people, for kings and all who are in authority, so that we may lead a tranquil and quiet life in all godliness and dignity." This passage underscores the importance of prayer in the lives of Christians, particularly in relation to those in positions of power and authority.

Prayer is foundational to the Christian faith and 1 Timothy 2:1-2 emphasizes the necessity of praying for leaders. This directive is rooted in the belief that God is sovereign and that He works through the prayers of His people to influence the affairs of nations. By praying for those in authority, believers acknowledge God's ultimate control and seek His guidance and wisdom for their leaders.

Praying for leaders has practical and spiritual implications. It fosters a spirit of peace and godliness within the community. When Christians pray for their leaders, they are asking God to grant them wisdom, discernment, and the ability to govern justly and righteously. This, in turn, contributes to a society where individuals can lead peaceful and quiet lives devoted to godliness and holiness.

Additionally, interceding for leaders aligns with the biblical call to love and serve others. It is an act of compassion and concern for the well-being of the nation and its people. By lifting leaders in prayer, Christians fulfill their role as intercessors, standing in the gap and seeking God's will for their country.

1 Timothy 2:1-2 calls Bible-believing evangelicals to prioritize prayer for those in authority. This practice not only aligns with God's command but also promotes peace, justice, and godliness in society.

How committed am I to this command? Well, for a few years, I held rallies in the political world. We did seven events and in total had 45,000 people in attendance. One of the parts of the conferences was about how faith has played a role in American history. I also talked about the need to pray for our leaders. Now, you must understand that these were essentially partisan events with ninety-nine percent of the people coming from one side of the aisle. Even though that was the case, I made sure that we prayed for all of our leaders, including some very famous people from the other side, who I prayed for by name. Imagine leading 10,000 people (our largest event) in praying by name for their main political rival. Do you know what is interesting though? You wouldn't believe how many people came up to me after the events and said something similar to, "Thank you for having us pray for those on the other side. I didn't like it at first, but you are right, we need to pray for all of our leaders. So, thank you."

Stories of Political Change Through Revival

Throughout history and in contemporary times, stories of political change through revival illustrate the transformative impact of prayer, moral leadership, and collective action.

Throughout American history revival movements have played a pivotal role in catalyzing significant moral and social reforms. These movements, often referred to as the Great Awakenings, have demonstrated the profound impact that spiritual renewal can have on society. The First and Second Great Awakenings, spanning from the early 18th to the mid-19th centuries, sparked widespread religious fervor and led to the emergence of movements advocating for abolitionism, labor rights, and temperance.

The abolitionist movement, which sought to end slavery in the United States, was profoundly influenced by the evangelical fervor of the Second Great Awakening. Evangelical preachers like Charles Finney and Theodore Weld emphasized the inherent dignity and equality of all people, drawing on biblical principles to argue against the institution of slavery. Their messages resonated with many Christians, who became active in the fight for abolition. This spiritual revival fueled a moral conviction that slavery was not only a social ill but also a profound sin against God, leading to the eventual emancipation of enslaved people and significant steps toward racial justice.

Similarly, the labor rights movement gained momentum from the same wave of evangelical revivalism. The harsh conditions faced by workers in factories and mines were increasingly viewed through the lens of Christian compassion and justice. Evangelicals advocated for fair wages, reasonable working hours, and safe working conditions, aligning their efforts with biblical calls for justice and care for the oppressed. The temperance movement, aimed at reducing alcohol consumption and its associated social problems, also found strong support among evangelicals who preached about the virtues of self-control and the dangers of intemperance.

The Civil Rights Movement of the 20th century is another powerful example of how Christian faith can drive societal transformation. Christian leaders like Martin Luther King Jr. drew deeply from their faith to advocate for racial justice and equality. King's vision of a "beloved community" was rooted in the biblical concept of agape love, which seeks the well-being of all people. Churches across the nation became centers of mobilization, organizing protests, marches, and voter registration drives. This movement, steeped in Christian principles of justice and love, led to significant legislative changes, such as the Civil Rights Act of 1964 and the Voting Rights Act of 1965, marking substantial progress toward equality.

Revival movements have demonstrated the profound capacity of spiritual renewal to catalyze societal transformation. From the abolitionist and labor rights movements in the United States to the

Civil Rights Movement and beyond, faith has consistently inspired and sustained efforts for justice and reform. By drawing on biblical principles and the power of the Holy Spirit, these movements have shown that genuine revival leads to lasting change, advancing God's purposes and bringing hope to a broken world.

Revival in government and politics is a call to align leadership and policies with biblical principles of justice, compassion, and integrity. By understanding the biblical perspective on government, acknowledging historical Christian influence, navigating contemporary challenges with faith and wisdom, engaging in the public square with courage and conviction, prioritizing prayer for national leaders, and learning from stories of political change through revival, Christians can contribute to societal renewal and advocate for policies that honor God and promote the flourishing of humanity. I hope this chapter inspires and equips believers to uphold righteousness in governance, pursue justice with humility, and engage in transformative practices that reflect the values of God's Kingdom in the public sphere.

Chapter Eight
Cultural Transformation through Revival

Cultural transformation through revival encompasses the profound impact of spiritual renewal on media, entertainment, social justice, and the arts. From an evangelical perspective, revival in these spheres involves recognizing the influence of media on societal values, embracing opportunities for Christian engagement, understanding biblical justice, and celebrating stories of societal reform catalyzed by spiritual awakening.

From a biblical perspective, the media and entertainment industry has increasingly become a cesspool of filth and anti-Christian propaganda, presenting significant challenges to those who seek to uphold biblical values. Long gone are films like Ben Hur and the Ten Commandments. Instead, modern media often glorifies lifestyles and behaviors that directly contradict the teachings of Scripture. Content that promotes sexual immorality, violence, and profanity is rampant, creating a cultural milieu that desensitizes viewers and normalizes sinful behavior. Christians would do well to remember Psalm 101:3-4:

I will set no worthless thing before my eyes;
I hate the work of those who fall away;
It shall not cling to me.
A perverse heart shall leave me;
I will know no evil.

Moreover, the entertainment industry frequently portrays Christianity and Christians in a negative light. Christians are often depicted as intolerant, ignorant, or hypocritical, reinforcing harmful stereotypes and fostering societal prejudice against those who hold to biblical convictions. This portrayal can discourage individuals from exploring or expressing their faith, particularly young people who are highly influenced by media representations.

The industry also propagates ideologies that undermine core Christian beliefs. Secularism, moral relativism, and materialism are prevalent themes, pushing a worldview where God is either irrelevant or nonexistent. Shows and movies often promote the idea that personal happiness and fulfillment come from self-indulgence and the pursuit of worldly success rather than a relationship with God and living according to His Word.

Despite this pervasive negativity, there is hope. Christians can choose to support and create wholesome, faith-affirming media. By advocating for and consuming content that aligns with biblical values, believers can influence the market and promote positive change. Additionally, engaging with media critically and discerningly, guided by prayer and scriptural principles, allows Christians to navigate this challenging landscape while maintaining their integrity and witness.

The Impact on Media and Entertainment

Media and entertainment hold significant power in shaping cultural norms, values, and worldviews. The pervasive influence of media narratives, pop culture, and ethical dilemmas presented in various forms of entertainment plays a crucial role in defining the moral and spiritual landscape of society. As Christians, it is essential to recognize this influence and engage thoughtfully with different forms of media to promote values that align with biblical principles.

Cultural Narratives

Media narratives have a profound impact on public opinion, attitudes toward morality, and perceptions of societal issues. Through news outlets, television shows, movies, and even social media platforms, media shapes the collective consciousness and behavior of society. Stories told through these mediums can either uplift and inspire or distort and mislead. Proverbs 4:23 advises, "Watch over your heart with all diligence, for from it flow the springs of life." This underscores the importance of being discerning about the media we consume, as it influences our hearts and minds.

For example, media coverage of social justice issues can raise awareness and mobilize action towards positive change. However, it can also perpetuate biases and misinformation. As Christians, we must seek truth and wisdom in our media consumption, aligning our perspectives with God's Word and not being swayed by the prevailing cultural winds. By critically evaluating media narratives, Christians can better understand how to engage with society in a way that reflects biblical values and promotes justice, mercy, and truth.

Pop Culture

Trends in music, film, television, and social media significantly impact how individuals perceive themselves, others, and the world around them. Pop culture often reflects and reinforces societal values, which can shape identity and behavior, particularly among younger generations. Romans 12:2 admonishes believers, "Do not be conformed to this world, but be transformed by the renewing of your mind." This call to nonconformity encourages Christians to resist adopting the world's values.

Music and movies, for instance, can profoundly affect emotions and attitudes. While some content promotes positive messages of love, hope, and perseverance, other content may glorify materialism, violence, or promiscuity. Social media, with its emphasis on appearance and instant gratification, can lead to issues such as low self-esteem, depression, and anxiety. As evangelicals, we are called to be salt and light in the world (Matthew 5:13-16), which includes being mindful of the cultural influences we embrace and propagate.

Engaging with pop culture from a biblical perspective involves both discernment and creativity. Christians are encouraged to create and support media that upholds biblical values, offering alternatives that inspire and uplift rather than degrade and corrupt. By doing so, believers can contribute to a cultural narrative that honors God and promotes the well-being of individuals and society as a whole.

Ethical Concerns

The immoral content presented in media, such as portrayals of violence, sexuality, and substance abuse, raises important questions about the impact of media content on moral development and societal well-being. Philippians 4:8 instructs, "Finally, brothers and sisters, whatever is true, whatever is honorable, whatever is right, whatever is pure, whatever is lovely, whatever is commendable, if there is any excellence and if anything worthy of praise, think about these things." This verse highlights the importance of focusing on content that edifies and encourages righteous living.

Excessive portrayals of violence in movies and video games can desensitize individuals to real-world suffering and contribute to aggressive behavior. Similarly, the normalization of promiscuity and substance abuse in media can lead to moral decay and societal harm. As Christians, it is vital to advocate for media that promotes healthy, virtuous lifestyles and to challenge content that undermines biblical principles.

Parents, in particular, have a responsibility to guide their children's media consumption, teaching them to discern and choose content wisely. By fostering a culture of critical engagement with media, Christians can help mitigate its negative effects and promote a society that values integrity, compassion, and godliness.

Media and entertainment profoundly influence cultural norms, values, and worldviews. From a Christian perspective, it is crucial to engage with media thoughtfully and discerningly, promoting narratives that align with biblical principles and challenging those that do not. By doing so, Christians can contribute to a culture that honors God and fosters the well-being of individuals and society. Through critical evaluation, creative engagement, and ethical advocacy, believers can navigate the media landscape in a way that reflects the love and truth of Christ.

Opportunities for Christians in Media and Arts— Influencing Culture and Promoting Biblical Values

Christian engagement in media and the arts offers unique opportunities to influence culture and promote biblical values. By focusing on creative excellence, redemptive storytelling, and cultural critique, believers can effectively shape societal norms and inspire spiritual transformation.

Creative Excellence

Producing media content that upholds excellence in storytelling, aesthetics, and moral integrity is essential for reflecting God's truth and beauty. Colossians 3:23 reminds us, "Whatever you do, do your work heartily, as for the Lord and not for people." This call to excellence applies to all endeavors, including media and the arts.

Creative excellence means crafting narratives that are compelling, well-produced, and ethically sound. It involves using the highest standards of artistic expression to convey messages that honor God and uplift viewers. When Christians commit to excellence in their creative work, they demonstrate the value of quality and integrity, setting a standard for others to follow. Moreover, excellence in media attracts a broader audience, providing more opportunities to share the gospel and biblical principles.

Christian artists and media professionals can excel in their fields by continually honing their skills, collaborating with others who share their commitment to quality, and seeking inspiration from Scripture and prayer. By doing so, they can create works that not only entertain but also provoke thought, inspire action, and reflect the character of God.

Redemptive Storytelling

Sharing stories of redemption, hope, and faith through various artistic mediums resonates with audiences and inspires spiritual transformation. Jesus frequently used parables—stories with profound moral and spiritual lessons—to teach and connect with people. In the same way, modern Christian storytellers can use their platforms to share powerful narratives that illustrate God's redemptive work.

Redemptive storytelling involves highlighting themes of forgiveness, restoration, and the triumph of good over evil. These stories offer a counter-narrative to the often cynical and despairing messages prevalent in mainstream media. By showcasing the transformative power of God's love and grace, Christian media can encourage viewers to seek spiritual renewal and deepen their faith.

Films like "The Chronicles of Narnia" series and "The Passion of the Christ" are examples of how redemptive storytelling can impact audiences. These works not only entertain but also convey profound spiritual truths that resonate with believers and non-believers alike. By embedding biblical themes into engaging and relatable stories, Christian media can bridge the gap between faith and culture, offering hope and inspiration to a diverse audience.

One of my most recent books demonstrates this principle perfectly. It is not a Christian book, per se. It is a book written by a Christian that portrays Christian principles. Called *Four Seasons*, it is the story of a billionaire who finds out he has terminal cancer and has one year—four seasons—left to live. One member of the cast of characters, one of the billionaire's daughters, is married to a young Presbyterian minister. Through that character, I am able to insert some Biblical thinking into the book. So, the book is appreciated by Christians, who recognize the lessons, and it is also appreciated by a wider audience because it isn't heavy-handed in its proclamation of the gospel.

Cultural Critique

Critically engaging with media narratives and offering alternative perspectives rooted in biblical truth and moral clarity is another vital aspect of Christian engagement in media and the arts. Romans 12:2 advises, "And do not be conformed to this world, but be transformed by the renewing of your mind." This transformation involves discerning and challenging the prevailing cultural narratives that contradict biblical values.

Cultural critique means analyzing and responding to media content from a biblical perspective. It involves identifying and addressing the underlying messages and values presented in films, television shows, music, and other media forms. By doing so, Christians can offer alternative viewpoints that highlight truth, justice, and righteousness. My main suggestion regarding this is to engage ourselves under the Biblical principle of "speaking the truth in love." (Ephesians 4:15)

Christian media critics and commentators play a crucial role in this process. Through reviews, articles, podcasts, and social media, they can help audiences navigate the complex media landscape, encouraging discernment and critical thinking. By highlighting both the positive and negative aspects of media content, they equip believers to make informed choices that align with their faith.

Moreover, offering alternative media content that upholds biblical values provides audiences with positive options. Christian filmmakers, musicians, and writers can create works that challenge the status quo and present a vision of a world transformed by God's love and truth.

Christian engagement in media and the arts is a powerful tool for influencing culture and promoting biblical values. By focusing on creative excellence, redemptive storytelling, and cultural critique, believers can shape societal norms, inspire spiritual transformation, and offer a compelling vision of God's Kingdom. Through their work, Christian artists and media professionals have the opportunity to reflect God's truth and beauty, share stories of hope and redemption, and critically engage with the cultural narratives of our time. In doing so, they contribute to a more just, compassionate, and spiritually enriched world.

I believe now more than ever that we should be engaged in cultural debates. The voice of Christians, informed by scriptures, should be one of the voices heard in determining the future of our country. Christian creative types should be pushing forward with their work to engage and influence the world around us.

Chapter Nine
How to Bring Revival to America

The Call to Action

Revival is not merely a historical phenomenon or a theoretical concept but a divine call to personal transformation, communal renewal, and national restoration. As believers, we are entrusted with the responsibility to seek God fervently, embody holiness in our lives, encourage our churches and communities, envision a future transformed by revival, and hold steadfast to the promises of God for a revived nation.

Up to this point, I have yet to tell you my personal story about revival. It started in 1983 in a small town outside of Seattle called North Bend, nestled in the foothills of the Cascade Mountains. It was there, in a small youth group of eight young students, of whom only one was actually Christian, that I saw revival come. Revival hit that youth group in a tiny Lutheran church called Mt Si Lutheran Church, at the corner of 8th and Ogle. It didn't hit the church, mind you, as many of the adults didn't know what to do with what came next.

Notice above I said that only one of the kids in our youth group was actually a Christian. Well, one summer, she went on vacation, and it was left to the seven not-yet-Christian kids to hold down the youth group. In July, a whole bunch of us and our friends went on a canoe retreat on Lake Chelan, one of the most beautiful lakes you will ever see, located in eastern Washington. There, nearly twenty kids gave their lives to Christ. We were on fire! Over the course of the next school year, my senior year, we saw hundreds of kids get saved, and we would regularly have 100 kids at our weekly Bible study—which we called

T.A.B.S. (Teenage Bible Study)—led by our fearless youth minister, Sam Samuelson. The biggest story in our high school the next year was what God was doing in this ragtag army of Christian kids. Many of us went to Bible college and then into ministry. That was the closest thing I have seen to true revival. What happened there continues in us today, through me writing this book and through many others, including a close friend of mine, Monty Wright, who went to Bible college with me, started a church with me, planted another church out of that church, and who now oversees hundreds of churches as a district superintendent of that denomination. Over 40 years later, the effects of that revival are still being felt.

I will never forget the moment that young woman, who was formerly the only Christian in that youth group, came back from vacation, saw an obvious difference in our lives, and stopped me to ask, "What in the world happened while I was gone?"

My answer was simple, "We all got saved!"

I have always looked back at that revival and the others I have researched and sought the answer to how we can bring about revival. I believe it starts with prayer and holiness from the hearts of hungry people.

Personal Commitment to Prayer and Holiness— Prayer as the Foundation of Revival

Prayer is essential in bringing about revival, acting as the spiritual catalyst that ignites and sustains transformative change. From a biblical perspective, revival is a profound awakening to God's presence, leading to repentance, renewal, and a deeper commitment to Christ. Prayer lays the groundwork for this by fostering a heart of humility and dependence on God.

Fervent Prayer: James 5:16 says, "A prayer of a righteous person, when it is brought about, can accomplish much." Personal and corporate prayer is essential for inviting God's presence, wisdom, and guidance into our lives, churches, and nation.

Through prayer, believers intercede for their communities, churches, and nations, asking God to pour out His Spirit and bring about a spiritual awakening. It aligns the hearts of the faithful with God's will, creating a collective yearning for His intervention and guidance. Historical revivals, such as the Great Awakenings, were preceded by fervent, united prayer, demonstrating its pivotal role.

Holiness and Repentance: Embracing a lifestyle of holiness and repentance prepares our hearts to receive God's blessings and empowers us to live as ambassadors of His Kingdom (1 Peter 1:15-16).

Prayer cultivates personal holiness and readiness to be instruments of revival. As individuals seek God earnestly, they experience personal renewal, becoming vessels through which God can work. This personal transformation spreads, leading to communal and national revival.

Seeking God's Face: Psalm 27:8 urges us to continuously look for the face of God, "When You said, 'Seek My face,' my heart said to You, 'I shall seek Your face, Lord.'" Revival begins with a deep longing for intimacy with God, surrendering our lives to His will, and interceding for spiritual awakening.

Prayer opens the door for divine encounters, miracles, and a heightened sense of God's presence. It breaks through worldly strongholds, allowing the gospel to penetrate hearts and minds with greater power and clarity. In essence, prayer is the lifeblood of revival, fueling the movement of God's Spirit and drawing people into a renewed relationship with Him.

I will say this: without a remnant of praying people, we will never see revival in our land. With a praying remnant, we place ourselves directly in the path of the oncoming revival!

Vision for the Future of America Through Revival— God's Sovereign Plan for Nations

2 Chronicles 7:14: "My people who are called by My name humble themselves, and pray and seek My face, and turn from their wicked ways, then I will hear from Heaven, and I will forgive their sin and will heal their land." God promises restoration and healing for nations that turn to Him in repentance and faith.

A Transformed Society: Envisioning America as a nation where righteousness, justice, compassion, and unity prevail, reflecting the values of God's Kingdom and bringing glory to His name. In such a vision, every aspect of life reflects biblical principles, with justice guiding laws and policies, compassion driving social programs, and unity fostering a spirit of togetherness among diverse communities. This transformed society would prioritize the well-being of all its members, uplift the marginalized, and uphold integrity and truth in all spheres of life. As believers, our goal is to contribute to this vision by living out our faith in practical ways, advocating for justice, and promoting love and reconciliation. Ultimately, this vision aims to bring glory to God's name by demonstrating His Kingdom on earth, fulfilling the call to be His representatives in a world that reflects His righteousness and grace.

Leadership and Governance: Praying for leaders at all levels of government involves asking God to grant them wisdom, integrity, and a commitment to policies that promote the common good. By seeking divine guidance, leaders can govern with fairness and uphold the principles of justice and mercy. This prayerful support ensures that decisions reflect God's values, fostering a society where policies are crafted with compassion and righteousness. Through such leadership, governments can address the needs of all citizens, uphold moral standards, and advance justice, aligning with biblical principles. By lifting our leaders in prayer, we contribute to a governance that honors God and works for the well-being of every individual, promoting a society that reflects His love and truth.

Hope for the Future—The Promises of God for a Revived Nation

Isaiah 58:11 states, "And the Lord will continually guide you, and satisfy your desire in scorched places, and give strength to your bones; and you will be like a watered garden, and like a spring of water whose waters do not fail." This verse offers a powerful promise from God that can profoundly impact our understanding of revival and its effects.

In the context of pursuing revival, this promise assures believers of God's continuous guidance, provision, and protection. Revival, marked by renewed spiritual fervor and commitment to God, brings a heightened sense of dependence on His promises. As we seek revival, this verse encourages us to trust that God will lead us through challenging times, represented metaphorically as "scorched places." The difficulties and trials of life do not deter God's provision; rather, they become the backdrop against which His faithfulness shines most brightly.

Trusting in God's promises means believing that His guidance is constant and His provision is abundant, even in the most trying circumstances. Revival brings a deepened awareness of God's presence, transforming our spiritual landscape into a "watered garden" where His grace and nourishment flow freely. This renewed spiritual vitality enables believers to be like "a spring of water whose waters never fail," continually refreshed and equipped to bear fruit.

As we pursue revival, this assurance of divine guidance and provision strengthens our faith, empowering us to face challenges with confidence and hope. By trusting in God's promises, we align our efforts with His will, experiencing the transformative power of His presence in every aspect of our lives and contributing to a revival that reflects His eternal faithfulness and love.

Psalm 85:6 asks, "Will You not revive us again, so that Your people may rejoice in You?" This heartfelt plea reflects a deep anticipation of God's faithfulness to restore and renew His people. This verse underscores the hopeful expectation that God will bring revival, leading to profound joy, peace, and spiritual abundance for our nation.

Anticipating God's revival involves trusting that He will answer the earnest prayers of His people, revitalizing their spiritual lives and transforming their communities. Revival is more than just a renewal of faith; it is a divine intervention that brings about a significant shift in collective spiritual health. It is an invitation for God to pour out His grace, igniting a fresh passion for Him and His purposes.

As we pray for revival, we anticipate that God will rejuvenate our spirits, bringing a renewed sense of joy and peace that comes from a deeper relationship with Him. This revival will not only revive individual hearts but will also ripple through our nation, fostering a culture of spiritual abundance where God's presence is tangibly felt.

The promise of revival in Psalm 85:6 assures us that God desires for His people to experience His joy and peace. It's a call to seek His face with the confidence that He will act in faithfulness. In response, our nation can be transformed into a place where spiritual vitality and divine blessing are evident, reflecting the profound impact of God's restorative power.

Final Exhortation to Pursue Revival

As we reflect on the call to pursue revival, it is crucial to understand that achieving such a spiritual awakening demands a bold and unwavering commitment. Revival is not merely a series of events or programs but a deep, transformative work of God that begins with the individual believer and extends to communities and nations. This pursuit involves several key elements: courageous faith and obedience, persistent prayer, and a steadfast commitment to holiness. Let us delve into these aspects with a view to how they can collectively contribute to a genuine and lasting revival.

Courageous Faith and Obedience

Joshua 1:9 provides a powerful mandate for believers, "Have I not commanded you? Be strong and courageous! Do not be terrified nor dismayed, for the Lord your God is with you wherever you go." This verse captures the essence of what it means to step out in faith. Revival requires believers to act with courage and confidence, knowing that God's presence is their strength and assurance.

Courageous faith is about more than just individual resolve; it involves boldly proclaiming the gospel in a world that often resists or mocks the message. It means standing firm in our convictions, sharing the transformative power of Christ, and contending for revival in our personal spheres of influence. Whether through personal conversations, public proclamations, or acts of service, we are called to be ambassadors of God's Kingdom. Romans 1:16 says, "For I am not ashamed of the gospel, for it is the power of God for salvation to everyone who believes."

Obedience plays a critical role here. Just as Joshua was commanded to lead with strength and faith, so too are we called to follow God's lead in our efforts for revival. This means aligning our actions with God's Word, being obedient to His call, and trusting Him to work through us. Our courage and obedience can ignite a spark that leads to a broader spiritual awakening as we faithfully live out and share the gospel.

Persistent Prayer

Persistent prayer is another cornerstone of pursuing revival. In Luke 18:1, Jesus teaches about the importance of persistent prayer, saying, "Now He was telling them a parable to show that at all times they ought to pray and not become discouraged." Revival is birthed through prayer, a continuous, earnest seeking of God's intervention and guidance.

Believers are called to engage in steadfast prayer, believing in God's power to bring about revival. This involves not only praying for our own needs but also interceding for others—our friends, family, communities, and the nation as a whole. Persistent prayer means lifting up prayers of repentance, asking for God's forgiveness and cleansing, and seeking His divine presence to revive and restore hearts.

Intercession also involves pleading for the spiritual awakening of our nation. As we see moral and social challenges in our society, our response should be to pray fervently for God's transformative work. God has promised that if His people humble themselves, pray, and seek His face, He will hear from Heaven and heal their land (2 Chronicles 7:14). Persistent prayer is a demonstration of our faith in this promise and our commitment to seeing God's Kingdom come.

Commitment to Holiness

A commitment to holiness is foundational for revival. 1 Peter 1:16 commands, "Because it is written: 'You shall be holy, for I am holy.'" Holiness is not merely about individual piety but encompasses living a life of integrity, humility, and reflection of Christ's character. It is through personal holiness that believers become vessels through which God can work powerfully.

Holiness involves more than avoiding sin; it includes embracing a lifestyle that honors God in all aspects—our thoughts, actions, and relationships. It requires a continual pursuit of righteousness and an earnest desire to reflect Christ's love, purity, and grace. When the church collectively commits to holiness, it creates an environment where revival can take root and flourish.

Furthermore, personal holiness fuels our witness. When believers live out their faith authentically, they draw others to the beauty and truth of the gospel. It's through a life of integrity and purity that we reflect God's character and make a compelling case for His transformative power.

Embracing the Call to Revival

Seeing revival in America requires a collective commitment to prayer, holiness, unity, and faith in God's promises. As believers, we must engage in fervent prayer, encourage our churches and communities, and envision a future transformed by revival. Holding onto hope in God's faithfulness, sharing inspiring stories of His work, and exhorting one another to pursue revival with courage and obedience align us with God's heart for spiritual awakening and national renewal.

I hope this chapter inspires and equips believers to embrace their role as catalysts for revival. By trusting in God's power to transform hearts, communities, and our nation, we participate in advancing His Kingdom and bringing glory to His name. As we step forward with faith, prayer, and holiness, let us believe in the profound impact of God's work through us, confident that He can bring about a revival that changes lives and renews our land for His glory.

Afterword
Utilizing Spiritual Disciplines for Personal and National Revival

Throughout this book I have talked about what Christians need to do to bring about revival, including prayer, worship, scripture reading and more. Yet, many Christians do not know how to go about these things and can feel overwhelmed. I want to share some thoughts on a book that helped shape my spiritual formation early on in my Christian life. In the pursuit of revival—both personal and national—Richard Foster's insights into spiritual disciplines offer a roadmap for cultivating a vibrant relationship with God, which is essential in seeing revival. These disciplines are not mere rituals but transformative practices that deepen our intimacy with God, align our hearts with His purposes, and prepare us to be agents of revival in our communities and country. I have long used Foster's teachings on spiritual disciplines to guide my spiritual life. I think you will find these thoughts on them enlightening and I hope you will dig into some more of Foster's books as a result. I believe that as we draw closer to God through spiritual disciplines, we put ourselves, and our nation in the path of the oncoming revival!

Understanding Spiritual Disciplines

Richard Foster, in his seminal work *Celebration of Discipline*, categorizes spiritual disciplines into three main groups: inward, outward, and corporate disciplines. Each category serves a unique purpose in nurturing our spiritual life and fostering revival.

The Inward Disciplines

Prayer: Prayer is the foundational discipline that underpins all spiritual growth and revival. Foster emphasizes various forms of prayer, including intercession, contemplation, and listening prayer. Through prayer, we cultivate intimacy with God, align our will with His, and experience His transforming presence. Personal revival begins with a dedicated prayer life, where we earnestly seek God's guidance, confess our sins, and surrender our lives to His will. In times of national need, fervent intercession becomes a powerful tool for inviting God's intervention and healing.

Meditation: Foster encourages meditation on Scripture and God's presence as a means to deepen our understanding of His Word and encounter His truth personally. Meditation involves reflecting deeply on Scripture, allowing its truths to penetrate our hearts, and applying them to our lives. Personal revival often emerges from moments of profound meditation where God's Word brings conviction, guidance, and assurance. Meditating on God's promises and character can also fuel our prayers for national revival, anchoring our petitions in His unchanging nature.

Fasting: Fasting is a discipline of abstaining from food or other comforts for a period to focus on prayer, repentance, and seeking God's direction. Foster highlights fasting as a means to humble ourselves before God, break the power of sinful habits, and intensify our spiritual hunger. In personal revival, fasting can serve as a catalyst for spiritual breakthroughs, deepening our dependence on God and aligning our hearts with His purposes. For national revival, fasting collectively as a church or nation demonstrates a unified cry for God's mercy and intervention.

The Outward Disciplines

Simplicity: Foster advocates for simplicity as a counter-cultural discipline that frees us from the grip of materialism and consumerism.

By intentionally living with less and focusing on what truly matters—God and His Kingdom—we cultivate a spirit of contentment, generosity, and stewardship. Personal revival often involves a reevaluation of our priorities and a deliberate pursuit of God's Kingdom over worldly pursuits. Embracing simplicity can also inspire societal change as Christians model a lifestyle of sacrificial love and generosity.

Solitude and Silence: In a world filled with noise and distractions, solitude and silence are disciplines that create space for us to hear God's voice and discern His will. Foster emphasizes withdrawing from busyness and external stimuli to cultivate intimacy with God, reflect on His Word, and receive His guidance. Personal revival often begins in moments of solitude and silence where God's presence becomes palpable, and His direction becomes clear. Cultivating these disciplines collectively can foster a culture of listening to God's voice and discerning His purposes for national revival.

Study: Studying God's Word is foundational to spiritual growth and revival. Foster encourages disciplined study of Scripture to deepen our understanding of God's character, His promises, and His will for our lives. Through systematic study, reflection, and application of Scripture, we gain spiritual insight, wisdom, and discernment. Personal revival is often fueled by a deep engagement with God's Word, as His truth transforms our minds and hearts, aligning them with His purposes. Studying Scripture collectively as a church or nation can also unify believers around God's truth and inspire concerted efforts toward national revival.

The Corporate Disciplines

Worship: Corporate worship, praise, and thanksgiving in community are central to Foster's vision of spiritual disciplines. These disciplines foster an atmosphere where God's presence is experienced, His Word is proclaimed, and believers are united in their devotion and commitment to God. In personal revival, worship and praise center our hearts on God, celebrating His goodness, faithfulness, and holiness. In a national context, corporate worship becomes a unifying force, bringing together believers from different backgrounds and denominations to seek God's face and intercede for His mercy and healing upon the nation.

Community: Foster emphasizes the importance of community in fostering spiritual growth and accountability. In community, believers encourage one another, support one another, and challenge one another to live out their faith. Personal revival often flourishes in the context of authentic community, where relationships are built on love, trust, and mutual respect. In a national context, a strong Christian community can serve as a beacon of hope and a catalyst for societal transformation, as believers work together to address social injustices, promote moral values, and demonstrate Christ's love to the world.

Service and Celebration: In Service and Celebration, Foster underscores the importance of serving others and celebrating God's goodness and faithfulness in community. Through acts of service, believers demonstrate Christ's love to others, meet practical needs, and bring hope to the broken and needy. In celebration, believers rejoice in God's work in their lives, their church, and their nation, giving thanks and glory to Him for His faithfulness and provision.

Applying Spiritual Disciplines for Personal and National Revival

The application of spiritual disciplines for personal and national revival begins with a commitment to intentional and consistent practice. Remember, reading about them doesn't change anything. Practicing them changes *all* things. Here are practical steps to cultivate these disciplines:

Personal Commitment: Make a personal commitment to prioritize spiritual disciplines in your daily life. Set aside dedicated time for prayer, meditation, study of Scripture, and fasting. Cultivate a habit of seeking God's presence and guidance in all aspects of your life.

Community Engagement: Engage actively in a Christian community where you can practice corporate disciplines such as worship, fellowship, and service. Join a local church that emphasizes spiritual growth and encourages accountability and mutual support among believers.

Leadership and Influence: If you are in a position of leadership or influence, model and promote the practice of spiritual disciplines within your sphere of influence. Encourage others to join you in prayer, fasting, and study of God's Word. Lead by example in demonstrating a life transformed by God's grace and truth.

Intercession for National Revival: Commit to fervent intercession for national revival, both individually and corporately. Pray for spiritual awakening, repentance, and transformation across the nation. Join prayer groups, participate in prayer gatherings, and seek opportunities to intercede for societal challenges and needs.

Living Out Revival: As you experience personal revival through spiritual disciplines, allow God's transformational work to overflow into your relationships, workplace, and community. Be a witness of God's love and truth through your words and actions, demonstrating the power and impact of revival in everyday life.

Richard Foster's teachings on spiritual disciplines provide a framework for experiencing personal revival and seeking national revival. They changed my spiritual life and the lives of many others. I believe they can change your life - and the life of our nation - as well. By cultivating a lifestyle of prayer, meditation, fasting, and study of Scripture—both individually and collectively—we prepare ourselves to be vessels of God's grace and agents of His Kingdom. As we engage in worship, community, service, and celebration, we demonstrate Christ's love to the world and invite others to experience the transforming power of God. May we embrace these disciplines wholeheartedly, trusting God to ignite revival in our hearts, our churches, and our nation for His glory and the advancement of His Kingdom.

Lessons From the Seven Churches of Revelation

The book of Revelation, the final book of the New Testament, contains letters to seven churches in Asia Minor. These letters, found in Revelation chapters 2 and 3, are messages from Christ Himself, delivered through the Apostle John. Each letter is both a commendation and a call to repentance and renewal, a divine blueprint for revival. This section explores these letters, emphasizing how Christ's words to these ancient churches provide timeless principles for personal, church, and national revival.

Ephesus: Returning to First Love

"To the angel of the church in Ephesus write: The One who holds the seven stars in His right hand, the One who walks among the seven golden lampstands, says this: 'I know your deeds and your labor and perseverance, and that you cannot tolerate evil people, and you have put those who call themselves apostles to the test, and they are not, and you found them to be false; and you have perseverance and have endured on account of My name, and have not become weary. But I have this against you, that you have left your first love. Therefore, remember from where you have fallen, and repent, and do the deeds you did at first; or else I am coming to you and I will remove your lampstand from its place—unless you repent.'" (Revelation 2:1-5, NASB)

The church at Ephesus was commendable for its hard work and doctrinal purity. Yet, it had abandoned its first love.

Revival Application

Revival begins with a return to our first love—Jesus Christ. As A.W. Tozer said, "What comes into our minds when we think about God is the most important thing about us." We must rekindle our passion for Christ, remembering the joy of our salvation and the love that initially drew us to Him. Personal revival requires repentance and a return to our first works—prayer, worship, and devotion.

Smyrna: Faithfulness in Persecution

"And to the angel of the church in Smyrna write: The first and the last, who was dead, and has come to life, says this: 'I know your tribulation and your poverty (but you are rich), and the slander by those who say they are Jews, and are not, but are a synagogue of Satan. Do not fear what you are about to suffer. Behold, the devil is about to throw some of you into prison, so that you will be tested, and you will have tribulation for ten days. Be faithful until death, and I will give you the crown of life.'" (Revelation 2:8-10, NASB)

Smyrna faced severe persecution, yet Christ encouraged them to remain faithful.

Revival Application

Revival often comes through trials. Persecution tests our faith and purifies our devotion. We must stand firm, trusting God's promises. As James 1:12 states, "Blessed is a man who perseveres under trial; for once he has been approved, he will receive the crown of life which the Lord has promised to those who love Him."

Pergamum: Rejecting Compromise

"**And to the angel of the church in Pergamum write**: The One who has the sharp two-edged sword says this: 'I know where you dwell, where Satan's throne is; and you hold firmly to My name, and did not deny My faith even in the days of Antipas, My witness, My faithful one, who was killed among you, where Satan dwells. But I have a few things against you, because you have some there who hold the teaching of Balaam, who kept teaching Balak to put a stumbling block before the sons of Israel, to eat things sacrificed to idols and to commit sexual immorality. So you too, have some who in the same way hold to the teaching of the Nicolaitans. Therefore repent; or else I am coming to you quickly, and I will wage war against them with the sword of My mouth.'" (Revelation 2:12-16, NASB)

Pergamum was a church that held firm in the face of external persecution but had compromised internally with false teachings and immoral practices.

Revival Application

Revival requires a rejection of compromise and a return to doctrinal purity and moral integrity. As Martyn Lloyd-Jones said, "When the church is absolutely different from the world, she invariably attracts it." We must guard against false teachings and sin, upholding the truth of God's Word.

Thyatira: Purity and Discipline

"**And to the angel of the church in Thyatira write**: The Son of God, who has eyes like a flame of fire, and feet like burnished bronze, says this: 'I know your deeds, and your love and faith, and service and perseverance, and that your deeds of late are greater than at first. But I have this against you, that you tolerate the woman Jezebel, who calls herself a prophetess, and she teaches and leads My bondservants astray so that they commit sexual immorality and eat things sacrificed to idols. I gave her time to repent, and she does not want to repent of her sexual immorality. Behold, I will throw her on a bed of sickness, and those who commit adultery with her into great tribulation, unless they repent of her deeds.'" (Revelation 2:18-22, NASB)

Thyatira was known for its love and service, yet it tolerated immorality and false prophecy. Dietrich Bonhoeffer warned, "Cheap grace is the preaching of forgiveness without requiring repentance, baptism without church discipline, communion without confession."

Revival Application

Revival necessitates church discipline and a commitment to purity. We must address sin within the church and call for repentance. As 1 Peter 4:17 states, "For it is time for judgment to begin with the household of God."

Sardis: Awakening the Dead

"**To the angel of the church in Sardis write**: He who has the seven spirits of God and the seven stars, says this: 'I know your deeds, that you have a name that you are alive, and yet you are dead. Be constantly alert, and strengthen the things that remain, which were about to die; for I have not found your deeds completed in the sight of My God. So remember what you have received and heard; and keep it, and repent. Then if you are not alert, I will come like a thief, and you will not know at what hour I will come to you.'" (Revelation 3:1-3, NASB)

Sardis had a reputation for being alive, but it was spiritually dead. Leonard Ravenhill stated, "The church is dying on its feet because it is not living on its knees." In America today you can find thousands of large church buildings filled with thousands of people, many of whom do not know God.

Revival Application

Revival in Sardis required awakening from spiritual slumber and returning to the foundational truths of the faith. We must assess the true spiritual state of our lives and churches, repenting of complacency and dead works. Genuine revival breathes life into what is spiritually dead.

Philadelphia: Persevering with Faith

"And to the angel of the church in Philadelphia write: He who is holy, who is true, who has the key of David, who opens and no one will shut, and who shuts and no one opens, says this: 'I know your deeds. Behold, I have put before you an open door which no one can shut, because you have a little power, and have followed My Word, and have not denied My name. Behold, I will make those of the synagogue of Satan, who say that they are Jews and are not, but lie—I will make them come and bow down before your feet, and make them know that I have loved you. Because you have kept My word of perseverance, I also will keep you from the hour of the testing, that hour which is about to come upon the whole world, to test those who live on the earth.'" (Revelation 3:7-10, NASB)

Philadelphia was a church of little strength, yet it remained faithful.

Revival Application

Faithfulness in the face of adversity is key to revival. We must persevere, keeping God's Word and affirming His name. As Galatians 6:9 encourages, "Let's not become discouraged in doing good, for in due time we will reap, if we do not become weary."

Laodicea: Overcoming Lukewarmness

"**To the angel of the church in Laodicea write**: The Amen, the faithful and true Witness, the Origin of the creation of God, says this: 'I know your deeds, that you are neither cold nor hot; I wish that you were cold or hot. So because you are lukewarm, and neither hot nor cold, I will vomit you out of My mouth. Because you say, 'I am rich, and have become wealthy, and have no need of anything,' and you do not know that you are wretched, miserable, poor, blind, and naked, I advise you to buy from Me gold refined by fire so that you may become rich, and white garments so that you may clothe yourself and the shame of your nakedness will not be revealed; and eye salve to apply to your eyes so that you may see." (Revelation 3:14-18, NASB)

Laodicea was a wealthy, self-sufficient church that had become lukewarm. They were blind to their true spiritual condition. Oswald J. Smith said, "The church that is man-managed instead of God-governed is doomed to failure."

Revival Application

Overcoming lukewarmness involves recognizing our true spiritual poverty and seeking Christ's riches. We must repent of self-sufficiency and materialism, seeking instead the spiritual wealth that comes from Christ. As James 4:8 exhorts, "Come close to God and He will come close to you."

The letters to the seven churches in Revelation serve as a mirror reflecting our own spiritual condition. They call us to repentance, faithfulness, and a fervent return to our first love. Revival begins when we take Christ's words to heart, allowing them to transform us personally, our churches corporately, and our nation collectively. As we heed these divine messages, we pave the way for a mighty move of God's Spirit, igniting a revival that can change the world.

The timeless truths found in Revelation's letters are as relevant today as they were in the first century. As we apply these principles, let us echo the prayer of Habakkuk: "Lord, I have heard the report about You, and I was afraid. Lord, revive Your work in the midst of the years, in the midst of the years make it known. In anger remember mercy" (Habakkuk 3:2, NASB). May we see a great revival in our time, to the glory of God.

31-Day Devotional for Personal, Church, and National Revival

Personal Revival (Days 1-10)

Day 1: Seeking God's Presence

Bible Passage:
"Create in me a clean heart, God, and renew a steadfast spirit within me." – Psalm 51:10 (NASB)

Thought for the Day:
Revival begins within each of us, with a sincere desire to seek God's presence and be transformed by Him. King David's plea in Psalm 51:10 reflects a deep yearning for personal renewal and purity. It's a humble acknowledgment of our need for God's intervention in our hearts. To experience revival, we must first invite God to cleanse us and renew our spirits, making our hearts pure and our spirits steadfast.

In our busy lives, it's easy to lose sight of God's presence. We can become distracted by the noise of the world and the demands of daily life. Yet, God is always near, ready to meet us where we are. Today, let us take a moment to quiet our hearts and seek Him earnestly. Let us ask Him to create in us pure hearts and renew our spirits so that we may experience the fullness of His presence and power.

Prayer:
Dear Heavenly Father, I come before You with a humble heart, asking for Your cleansing and renewal. Create in me a pure heart and renew a

steadfast spirit within me. Help me to seek Your presence daily and to be transformed by Your love and grace. In Jesus' name, I pray. Amen.

Action Point:
Set aside a quiet time today, even if it's just for a few minutes, to be alone with God. Read Psalm 51:10 again, meditate on its meaning, and invite God to cleanse your heart and renew your spirit. Write down any thoughts or impressions that come to you during this time.

Day 2: Confession and Repentance

Bible Passage:
"If we confess our sins, He is faithful and righteous, so that He will forgive us our sins and cleanse us from all unrighteousness." – 1 John 1:9 (NASB)

Thought for the Day:
Confession and repentance are foundational to experiencing personal revival. In 1 John 1:9, we are assured of God's faithfulness and justice when we come to Him with a repentant heart. Confession involves acknowledging our sins before God, while repentance goes a step further—it's a turning away from sin and a turning toward God. As we confess our sins, God forgives us and purifies us, restoring our fellowship with Him and empowering us to live in His righteousness.

Today, reflect on your life and invite the Holy Spirit to reveal any areas where confession and repentance are needed. God desires honesty and humility from us. Confess any known sins to Him, trusting in His promise to forgive and cleanse you completely.

Prayer:
Heavenly Father, I confess my sins to You today. I acknowledge the ways I have fallen short of Your glory. Thank You for Your faithfulness and justice in forgiving me. Please purify my heart and empower me to walk in Your ways. In Jesus' name, I pray. Amen.

Action Point:
Take time to journal or silently reflect on areas in your life where confession and repentance are needed. Write down specific sins or patterns of behavior that you need to bring before God. Surrender these to Him and commit to making any necessary changes with His help.

Day 3: Renewing the Mind

Bible Passage:
"Do not be conformed to this world, but be transformed by the renewing of your mind, so that you may prove what the will of God is, that which is good and acceptable and perfect." – Romans 12:2 (NASB)

Thought for the Day:
Renewing our minds is essential for personal revival. In Romans 12:2, Paul encourages us not to be shaped by the values and attitudes of the world around us but to undergo a transformation through the renewing of our minds. This transformation enables us to discern and embrace God's will, which is always good, pleasing, and perfect. As we immerse ourselves in God's Word and align our thoughts with His truth, our minds are renewed, and we begin to think and act according to His purposes.

Today, consider the thoughts and beliefs that govern your mind. Are they aligned with God's Word, or have they been influenced by worldly perspectives? Ask the Holy Spirit to help you identify any areas where your thinking needs renewal. Allow Him to reshape your thoughts and attitudes according to His truth and wisdom.

Prayer:
Heavenly Father, I pray for a renewal of my mind today. Help me to reject the patterns of this world and to embrace Your truth. Transform my thinking so that I may understand Your will more clearly and follow it wholeheartedly. Thank You for Your Word, which guides and enlightens me. In Jesus' name, I pray. Amen.

Action Point:
Commit to daily reading and meditation on Scripture to renew your mind. Choose a passage from the Bible that speaks to an area of your life where you need transformation. Write down key verses and meditate on them throughout the day, asking God to renew your mind and align your thoughts with His truth.

Day 4: Restoring First Love

Bible Passage:
"But I have this against you, that you have left your first love. Therefore, remember from where you have fallen, and repent, and do the deeds you did at first." – Revelation 2:4-5a (NASB)

Thought for the Day:
In Revelation 2:4-5, Jesus addresses the church in Ephesus, admonishing them for losing their first love for Him. This passage serves as a poignant reminder to examine our own hearts and relationship with God. Just as earthly relationships can grow cold without intentional effort, so too can our love for God wane if not nurtured. Revival begins with a return to our first love—rekindling the passion and devotion we once had for Christ.

Today, take a moment to reflect on your journey with God. Have you drifted from the fervent love and zeal you once had for Him? Allow the Holy Spirit to reveal any areas where your love for God has grown cold. Repent and commit to doing the things you did at first—seeking Him eagerly, spending time in His Word, and communing with Him in prayer.

Prayer:
Lord Jesus, forgive me for allowing my love for You to grow cold. I repent and ask for Your forgiveness. Help me to rediscover the passion and devotion I once had for You. Stir my heart to seek You earnestly and to prioritize my relationship with You above all else. In Your name, I pray. Amen.

Action Point:
Make a list of activities or practices that helped cultivate your love for God when you first became a believer. Choose one of these practices and incorporate it back into your daily routine. Whether it's journaling your prayers, memorizing Scripture, or worshiping through music, commit to nurturing your relationship with God intentionally.

Day 5: Daily Surrender

Bible Passage:
"I have been crucified with Christ; and it is no longer I who live, but Christ lives in me; and the life which I now live in the flesh I live by faith in the Son of God, who loved me and gave Himself up for me." – Galatians 2:20 (NASB)

Thought for the Day:
Galatians 2:20 encapsulates the essence of daily surrender to Christ. As believers, we are called to allow Christ to live through us. Surrender is not a one-time event but a daily, ongoing commitment to submit our will, desires, and plans to God. It requires us to relinquish control and trust in His wisdom and guidance. When we surrender to Christ, His life and love flow through us, transforming our thoughts, actions, and attitudes.

Today, reflect on your own surrender to Christ. Are there areas of your life where you struggle to relinquish control? Surrender them to God in prayer. Ask the Holy Spirit to empower you to live by faith in Christ, trusting His promises and following His lead in every aspect of your life.

Prayer:
Heavenly Father, I surrender myself to You afresh today. I acknowledge that apart from You, I can do nothing. Thank You for the sacrifice of Your Son, Jesus Christ, who gave Himself for me. Help me to live by faith in Him, allowing His life to be expressed through mine. May Your will be done in my life today and always. In Jesus' name, I pray. Amen.

Action Point:
Identify one area of your life where you find it difficult to surrender control to God (e.g., relationships, career, finances). Write a prayer committing this area to God's sovereignty and asking for strength to trust Him completely. Throughout the day, whenever worry or doubt arises, recite this prayer and reaffirm your surrender to God's plan and purpose.

Day 6: Walking in the Spirit

Bible Passage:
"But I say, walk by the Spirit, and you will not carry out the desire of the flesh." – Galatians 5:16 (NASB)

Thought for the Day:
Galatians 5:16 urges us to walk by the Spirit, emphasizing the contrast between following the Holy Spirit's guidance and indulging in sinful desires. Walking in the Spirit means aligning our thoughts, actions, and decisions with God's will, empowered by His Spirit within us. It requires a conscious choice to surrender to His leadership, seeking His wisdom and strength in every situation. When we walk in the Spirit, we experience freedom from the bondage of sin and fulfillment from living according to God's purpose for our lives.

Today, examine your daily walk with God. Are there areas where you have been relying on your own strength rather than depending on the Holy Spirit? Surrender those areas to God and invite the Spirit to guide you. Ask Him to fill you afresh and empower you to live in obedience and holiness.

Prayer:
Heavenly Father, I thank You for the gift of Your Holy Spirit. Today, I choose to walk by the Spirit and not gratify the desires of the flesh. Fill me with Your Spirit's power and wisdom. Help me to discern Your voice and follow Your guidance in all that I do. May my life be a testimony of Your transforming work. In Jesus' name, I pray. Amen.

Action Point:
Throughout the day, practice listening to the Holy Spirit's promptings. Before making decisions or responding to situations, pause and ask for His guidance. Choose to obey His leading, even if it requires stepping out of your comfort zone or letting go of control. Keep a journal of moments where you sensed the Spirit's guidance and reflect on how following Him impacted your day.

Day 7: Fervent Prayer

Bible Passage:
"Therefore, confess your sins to one another, and pray for one another so that you may be healed. A prayer of a righteous person, when it is brought about, can accomplish much." – James 5:16 (NASB)

Thought for the Day:
James 5:16 highlights the potency of fervent prayer in the life of a believer. Prayer is not merely a ritualistic practice but a powerful means of communicating with God, seeking His will, and experiencing His healing and transformation. Fervent prayer involves earnestness, persistence, and faith in God's ability to answer according to His perfect purpose. It strengthens our relationship with God, aligns our hearts with His, and brings about spiritual healing and renewal.

Today, consider the role of prayer in your life. Are your prayers characterized by fervency and faith? Reflect on areas where you may need healing—whether spiritual, emotional, or physical—and bring them before God in prayer. Trust that He hears your prayers and will respond according to His wisdom and love.

Prayer:
Heavenly Father, thank You for the privilege of prayer. Today, I come before You with a humble heart, confessing my sins and seeking Your healing touch. I believe in the power of fervent prayer and ask for Your guidance and provision in my life. Strengthen my faith and help me to pray according to Your will. In Jesus' name, I pray. Amen.

Action Point:
Commit to setting aside dedicated time for prayer each day this week. Create a prayer list that includes personal needs, the needs of others, and praises for God's faithfulness. Spend intentional moments in prayer, focusing on each item on your list and trusting God to work in every situation. Note any specific answers or insights you receive during your prayer time.

Day 8: Holy Living

Bible Passage:
"But like the Holy One who called you, be holy yourselves also in all your behavior; because it is written: 'You shall be holy, for I am holy.'"
– 1 Peter 1:15-16 (NASB)

Thought for the Day:
In 1 Peter 1:15-16, Peter exhorts believers to live holy lives, reflecting the character of God who called them. Holiness is not about perfection but about a lifestyle marked by obedience to God's Word, purity of heart, and separation from sinful practices. As followers of Christ, our identity is rooted in His holiness, and we are called to emulate His example in every aspect of our lives. Personal revival involves a continual pursuit of holiness, allowing God to transform us from within and sanctify us for His purposes.

Today, consider how you can live a more holy life before God. Are there areas where compromise or sin has crept in? Surrender those areas to God and ask for His strength to live in obedience and purity. Let His Word guide your thoughts, actions, and choices as you strive to honor Him in all you do.

Prayer:
Heavenly Father, I desire to live a life that honors You and reflects Your holiness. Forgive me for times when I have strayed from Your path. Help me to walk in obedience and purity, guided by Your Word

and empowered by Your Spirit. May my life be a testimony of Your transforming grace. In Jesus' name, I pray. Amen.

Action Point:
Identify one area of your life where you need to make adjustments to align more closely with God's call to holiness (e.g., speech, entertainment choices, relationships). Write down practical steps you can take to honor God in that area. Commit to implementing these steps with God's help, trusting Him to strengthen you and guide you towards greater holiness each day.

Day 9: Hungering for God's Word

Bible Passage:
"But He answered and said, 'It is written: "Man shall not live on bread alone, but on every word that comes out of the mouth of God."'" – Matthew 4:4 (NASB)

Thought for the Day:
In Matthew 4:4, Jesus affirms the importance of God's Word as essential nourishment for our spiritual lives. Just as our bodies require food for sustenance, our souls hunger for the truth and wisdom found in Scripture. Hungering for God's Word involves a deep longing to know Him more intimately, to understand His will, and to align our lives with His purposes. It requires a daily commitment to study, meditate on, and apply Scripture, allowing it to shape our thoughts and actions.

Today, evaluate your hunger for God's Word. Are you actively seeking His truth through Scripture, or have you become complacent in your spiritual intake? Set aside time to immerse yourself in God's Word, allowing His truth to penetrate your heart and renew your mind. Let Scripture be your guide and source of strength as you pursue personal revival.

Prayer:
Heavenly Father, Your Word is a lamp to my feet and a light for my path. Today, I confess my hunger for Your truth and wisdom. Help me to prioritize time in Your Word, seeking to know You more deeply and to align my life with Your will. Open my heart and mind to receive Your Word afresh today. In Jesus' name, I pray. Amen.

Action Point:
Commit to a daily reading plan or study of Scripture. Choose a book of the Bible or a specific theme to explore over the next week. Set aside a designated time each day for reading and reflecting on Scripture, allowing God to speak to you through His Word. Consider journaling insights or verses that stand out to you during this time of study.

Day 10: Trusting in God's Promises

Bible Passage:
"Trust in the Lord with all your heart and do not lean on your own understanding. In all your ways acknowledge Him, and He will make your paths straight." – Proverbs 3:5-6 (NASB)

Thought for the Day:
Proverbs 3:5-6 is a timeless reminder of the importance of trusting God completely. Trust involves relinquishing our own understanding and relying on God's wisdom and guidance. When we trust in God's promises, we acknowledge His sovereignty and goodness, believing that He will direct our paths and fulfill His purposes for our lives. In times of uncertainty or difficulty, trusting in God's promises brings peace, assurance, and strength to persevere.

Today, reflect on the areas of your life where trust in God's promises may be lacking. Are there circumstances causing you to doubt or fear? Surrender those concerns to God and choose to trust Him wholeheartedly. Submit every aspect of your life to His will and seek His guidance in prayer, knowing that He is faithful to guide and provide for His children.

Prayer:
Heavenly Father, I confess my tendency to rely on my own understanding rather than trusting in You completely. Today, I choose to trust in Your promises and submit my life to Your will. Strengthen my faith and help me to follow Your guidance with confidence. Thank You for Your faithfulness and love. In Jesus' name, I pray. Amen.

Action Point:
Identify one specific promise from God in Scripture that you need to trust more fully (e.g., provision, guidance, peace). Write down this promise and memorize it. Whenever doubt or anxiety arises, recite this promise aloud and meditate on its truth. Trust God to fulfill His promise in His perfect timing and according to His perfect plan for your life.

Church Revival (Days 11-20)

Day 11: Unity in the Body

Bible Passage:
"[Be] diligent to keep the unity of the Spirit in the bond of peace." – Ephesians 4:3 (NASB)

Thought for the Day:
Ephesians 4:3 emphasizes the importance of unity within the Body of Christ. Unity is not merely the absence of conflict but the active pursuit of peace and harmony among believers. It requires humility, love, and a commitment to Christ-centered relationships. When the church is united in purpose and spirit, it reflects the unity of the triune God and becomes a powerful witness to the world. Church revival begins with unity, as it fosters spiritual growth, effective ministry, and a vibrant testimony of God's love.

Today, reflect on the state of unity within your church community. Are there divisions or misunderstandings that need reconciliation? Pray for unity among believers, asking the Holy Spirit to heal relationships and unite hearts in Christ-like love. Seek opportunities to foster unity by extending grace, resolving conflicts biblically, and prioritizing unity in prayer and fellowship.

Prayer:
Heavenly Father, Your Word calls us to keep the unity of the Spirit through the bond of peace. Today, I pray for unity within my church family. Help us to love one another deeply, to bear with one another in love, and to pursue peace in all circumstances. May our unity be a testimony of Your transforming power and draw others to know You. In Jesus' name, I pray. Amen.

Action Point:
Reach out to a fellow church member this week whom you may have had a misunderstanding with or haven't connected with in a while. Initiate a conversation of reconciliation, seeking to understand their perspective and extend forgiveness and grace where needed. Commit to praying regularly for unity within your church and look for ways to actively contribute to a spirit of unity among believers.

Day 12: Love for One Another

Bible Passage:
"I am giving you a new commandment, that you love one another; just as I have loved you, that you also love one another. By this all people will know that you are My disciples: if you have love for one another."
– John 13:34-35 (NASB)

Thought for the Day:
In John 13:34-35, Jesus gives His disciples a new commandment—to love one another as He has loved them. This love is not superficial or conditional but sacrificial and selfless, modeled after Christ's own love for us. Loving one another is not optional for followers of Christ; it is a defining characteristic that sets us apart and demonstrates our allegiance to Him. When the church embodies Christ-like love, it becomes a powerful testimony of His grace and draws others to Him.

Today, consider how you demonstrate love within your church community. Are there ways you can show Christ-like love more intentionally to those around you? Reflect on the sacrificial love of Jesus and ask the Holy Spirit to empower you to love others genuinely and selflessly, just as He loves you.

Prayer:
Dear Lord Jesus, thank You for Your commandment to love one another. Help me to love others as You have loved me—sacrificially, unconditionally, and without reserve. Show me opportunities to demonstrate Your love within my church and community. May my actions and words reflect Your grace and draw others closer to You. In Your name, I pray. Amen.

Action Point:
Choose one person within your church community whom you find challenging to love or connect with. Pray for that person daily this week, asking God to soften your heart and show you how you can demonstrate Christ's love to them. Look for practical ways to serve and encourage them, seeking reconciliation if needed, and strive to cultivate a spirit of unity and love within your church family.

Day 13: Faithful Preaching

Bible Passage:
"Preach the Word; be ready in season and out of season; correct, rebuke, and exhort, with great patience and instruction." – 2 Timothy 4:2 (NASB)

Thought for the Day:
In 2 Timothy 4:2, Paul charges Timothy to preach the Word faithfully, emphasizing the importance of proclaiming God's truth regardless of circumstances. Faithful preaching involves preparation, courage, and a commitment to speaking God's Word with clarity and conviction. It includes teaching, correcting, rebuking, and encouraging, all grounded in patience and careful adherence to Scripture. When the

church prioritizes faithful preaching, it equips believers for spiritual growth, challenges them to live according to God's standards, and fosters unity and maturity within the Body of Christ.

Today, reflect on the role of preaching in your church. Are you receiving biblical teaching that challenges and nurtures your faith? Pray for your church's pastors and leaders, asking God to grant them wisdom, boldness, and spiritual discernment as they proclaim His Word. Commit to actively engaging with and applying the teachings you receive, allowing God's Word to transform your life.

Prayer:
Heavenly Father, thank You for Your Word, which is a lamp to our feet and a light to our path. I pray for faithful preaching in my church— teaching that is rooted in Your truth, bold in its proclamation, and transformative in its impact. Grant our pastors and leaders wisdom and discernment as they prepare and deliver Your Word. Open our hearts to receive Your truth and empower us to live according to Your will. In Jesus' name, I pray. Amen.

Action Point:
Take time this week to reflect on the recent sermons or teachings you have heard. Identify one key message or biblical truth that stood out to you. Journal about how this truth can be applied to your life and commit to discussing it with a friend or family member to deepen your understanding and encourage one another in faithfulness.

Day 14: Spirit-Filled Worship

Bible Passage:
"But a time is coming, and even now has arrived, when the true worshipers will worship the Father in spirit and truth; for such people the Father seeks to be His worshipers. God is spirit, and those who worship Him must worship in spirit and truth." – John 4:23-24 (NASB)

Thought for the Day:
In John 4:23-24, Jesus teaches about the essence of true worship—worshiping the Father in spirit and truth. Spirit-filled worship goes beyond rituals and forms; it involves a heart surrendered to God, guided by His Spirit, and grounded in His truth. As believers, our worship should be authentic, characterized by reverence, adoration, and a deep desire to honor God in every aspect of our lives. When the church engages in spirit-filled worship, it invites God's presence, fosters unity, and magnifies His glory.

Today, consider your approach to worship in your church. Are you engaging with God in spirit and truth, or is worship merely a routine? Reflect on the sincerity of your worship and ask the Holy Spirit to deepen your reverence and love for God. Seek to worship Him in every area of your life, surrendering your heart and desires to His will.

Prayer:
Heavenly Father, I desire to worship You in spirit and in truth, with all my heart, soul, and mind. Fill me afresh with Your Holy Spirit, guiding my worship and transforming my heart to align with Your will. May my worship be pleasing to You and draw me closer to Your presence. In Jesus' name, I pray. Amen.

Action Point:
Prepare for worship this coming Sunday by spending time in prayer and reflection beforehand. Ask God to prepare your heart to worship Him sincerely and authentically. During the worship service, actively engage with the songs and prayers, focusing on the lyrics and their meaning. Seek to respond to God's presence and lead throughout the service, allowing His Spirit to minister to you and guide your worship experience.

Day 15: Discipleship and Mentoring

Bible Passage:
"Go, therefore, and make disciples of all the nations, baptizing them in the name of the Father and the Son and the Holy Spirit, teaching them to follow all that I commanded you; and behold, I am with you always, to the end of the age." – Matthew 28:19-20 (NASB)

Thought for the Day:
In Matthew 28:19-20, often called the Great Commission, Jesus commissions His disciples to make disciples of all nations. This mandate is not just about evangelism but also about discipleship—teaching new believers to obey everything Jesus commanded. Discipleship involves intentional relationships where mature believers guide and mentor others in their faith journey, helping them grow in their character, knowledge of God's Word, and obedience to Christ. Church revival flourishes when discipleship is prioritized, as it fosters spiritual maturity, unity, and the multiplication of committed followers of Jesus.

Today, reflect on your role in discipleship within your church community. Are you actively involved in mentoring others or being mentored yourself? Pray for God's guidance in identifying someone whom you can disciple or who can disciple you. Commit to investing in a relationship where spiritual growth and obedience to Christ are encouraged and nurtured.

Prayer:
Heavenly Father, thank You for the privilege of participating in Your Kingdom work through discipleship. Help me to obey Your command to make disciples, teaching them to follow You wholeheartedly. Show me someone whom I can mentor and guide in their faith journey. Grant me wisdom, patience, and love as I invest in their spiritual growth. In Jesus' name, I pray. Amen.

Action Point:
Reach out to a fellow believer in your church who may benefit from discipleship or mentoring. Offer to pray together regularly, study the

Bible together, or discuss spiritual topics. Be intentional about sharing your faith journey and encouraging each other to apply God's Word in daily life. Seek opportunities to meet consistently and support one another in pursuing greater obedience and devotion to Christ.

Day 16: Persistent Prayer

Bible Passage:
"They were continually devoting themselves to the apostles' teaching and to fellowship, to the breaking of bread and to prayer." – Acts 2:42 (NASB)

Thought for the Day:
Acts 2:42 provides a snapshot of the early church's devotion to prayer as a vital component of their fellowship and spiritual growth. Persistent prayer is more than a routine; it is a continual, earnest pursuit of God's presence and guidance. It involves consistent communication with God, seeking His will, and aligning our hearts with His purposes. When the church prioritizes persistent prayer, it opens doors for God's power to move, for hearts to be transformed, and for revival to ignite among God's people.

Today, consider your commitment to prayer within your church community. Are you actively engaged in praying for your church, its leaders, and its mission? Dedicate time to intercede fervently for spiritual renewal and revival within your congregation. Pray for unity, spiritual growth, and an outpouring of God's Spirit upon your church, trusting that He hears and answers prayers offered in faith.

Prayer:
Heavenly Father, I thank You for the privilege of prayer, through which we can seek Your face and align our hearts with Your will. Today, I pray for my church community. May we be devoted to prayer, seeking Your guidance, wisdom, and power. Stir our hearts to intercede persistently for revival and spiritual awakening. May Your Kingdom come, and Your will be done in our midst. In Jesus' name, I pray. Amen.

Action Point:
Commit to establishing a regular prayer routine specifically focused on your church's revival and spiritual growth. Set aside dedicated time each day to pray for your pastors, church leaders, ministries, and fellow church members. Keep a prayer journal to record specific requests and answers to prayer. Look for opportunities to participate in corporate prayer gatherings or prayer initiatives within your church, contributing to a culture of persistent prayer and dependence on God's guidance and provision.

Day 17: Generosity and Sharing

Bible Passage:
"And the congregation of those who believed were of one heart and soul; and not one of them claimed that anything belonging to him was his own, but all things were common property to them. And with great power the apostles were giving testimony to the resurrection of the Lord Jesus, and abundant grace was upon them all. For there was not a needy person among them, for all who were owners of land or houses would sell them and bring the proceeds of the sales and lay them at the apostles' feet, and they would be distributed to each to the extent that any had need." – Acts 4:32-35 (NASB)

Thought for the Day:
Acts 4:32-35 paints a picture of the early church's unity and generosity. They shared their possessions freely, ensuring that no one among them lacked basic necessities. Their generosity was a powerful demonstration of God's grace and love at work within the community of believers. Generosity is not just about financial giving but about a heart attitude that values others' needs above personal comfort or gain. When the church practices generosity and sharing, it fosters unity, meets practical needs, and provides a tangible witness of God's provision and care.

Today, reflect on your attitude towards generosity within your church community. Are you willing to share your time, resources, and talents with others? Ask God to reveal areas where you can be more generous and sacrificial in meeting the needs of those around you. Seek opportunities to give joyfully and cheerfully, knowing that God blesses a generous heart and uses it to build His Kingdom.

Prayer:
Heavenly Father, thank You for Your abundant blessings in my life. Help me to cultivate a generous heart, willing to share with others as You have generously shared with me. Show me practical ways I can bless and support my church community and those in need around me. May my giving reflect Your love and grace to others. In Jesus' name, I pray. Amen.

Action Point:
Identify one specific way you can practice generosity and sharing within your church community this week. It could be offering to help someone in need, contributing financially to a church initiative, or volunteering your time for a ministry project. Act on this opportunity with a joyful heart, trusting God to use your generosity to bless others and contribute to the revival and unity of your church.

Day 18: Bold Evangelism

Bible Passage:
"But you will receive power when the Holy Spirit has come upon you; and you shall be My witnesses both in Jerusalem and in all Judea, and Samaria, and as far as the remotest part of the earth." – Acts 1:8 (NASB)

Thought for the Day:
Acts 1:8 records Jesus' commission to His disciples, promising them the power of the Holy Spirit for the purpose of spreading the gospel boldly. Bold evangelism is fueled by the Holy Spirit's power and involves proclaiming the good news of Jesus Christ with courage and conviction. It requires stepping out of comfort zones, engaging with others about faith, and trusting God to work through our witness to draw people to Himself. When the church embraces bold evangelism,

it fulfills its mission to make disciples and spread God's Kingdom on earth.

Today, consider your role in sharing the gospel within your community and beyond. Are you actively seeking opportunities to share your faith with others? Pray for boldness and sensitivity to the leading of the Holy Spirit in your interactions with people who need to hear about Jesus. Ask God to use you as His instrument of love and truth, bringing others into a relationship with Him through your witness.

Prayer:
Heavenly Father, thank You for the privilege of sharing the gospel with others. Fill me with Your Holy Spirit and empower me to be a bold witness for Christ in my daily life. Open doors for meaningful conversations about faith and grant me wisdom to communicate Your love and truth effectively. May Your Spirit work through me to bring revival and transformation in the lives of those who hear Your Word. In Jesus' name, I pray. Amen.

Action Point:
Commit to praying daily for opportunities to share the gospel with at least one person in your life—whether a family member, friend, coworker, or neighbor. Look for natural openings in conversations or intentional moments to initiate discussions about faith. Be prepared to share your personal testimony of how Jesus has impacted your life and invite others to experience His love and salvation. Trust God to guide these interactions and use your boldness in evangelism to bring about revival in hearts and communities.

Day 19: Healing and Restoration

Bible Passage:
"Is anyone among you sick? Then he must call for the elders of the church and they are to pray over him, anointing him with oil in the name of the Lord; and the prayer of faith will restore the one who is

sick, and the Lord will raise him up, and if he has committed sins, they will be forgiven him." – James 5:14-15 (NASB)

Thought for the Day:
James 5:14-15 emphasizes the importance of prayer for healing and restoration within the church community. Healing is not only physical but also spiritual and emotional. As believers, we are called to pray earnestly for one another's healing, trusting in God's power to intervene according to His will. When the church engages in fervent prayer for healing and restoration, it demonstrates God's compassion, strengthens faith, and contributes to the spiritual revival of individuals and the community as a whole.

Today, reflect on the role of healing and restoration in your church's life. Are there individuals who need prayer for physical, emotional, or spiritual healing? Lift them up to God in prayer, believing in His ability to bring about transformation and renewal. Seek to participate actively in praying for and supporting those who are in need of healing, showing Christ's love and care through your actions.

Prayer:
Heavenly Father, I come before You with faith, believing in Your power to heal and restore. I lift up those in my church community who are sick or hurting—physically, emotionally, or spiritually. May Your healing touch be upon them, bringing comfort, strength, and restoration. Grant wisdom to our church leaders as they pray and anoint the sick. Use our prayers to demonstrate Your love and power, bringing glory to Your name. In Jesus' name, I pray. Amen.

Action Point:
Reach out to someone in your church who is facing a health challenge or personal struggle. Offer to pray with them specifically for healing and restoration, trusting God to work in their situation. Consider organizing a prayer gathering or small group focused on interceding for healing within your church community. Encourage others to participate and witness the power of God at work through collective prayer for healing and restoration.

Day 20: Living Out the Gospel

Bible Passage:
"Whatever you do in word or deed, do everything in the name of the Lord Jesus, giving thanks through Him to God the Father." – Colossians 3:17 (NASB)

Thought for the Day:
Colossians 3:17 encapsulates the essence of living out the gospel in our daily lives. As followers of Christ, everything we say and do should reflect His character and honor His name. Whether at home, work, school, or in our communities, our words and actions should be infused with gratitude and a desire to glorify God. Living out the gospel means embodying Christ's love, truth, and compassion in all interactions, serving as ambassadors of His Kingdom wherever we go. When the church collectively lives out the gospel, it becomes a powerful witness of God's transformative work and invites others to experience His grace and salvation.

Today, examine your life in light of Colossians 3:17. Are there areas where your words or actions do not align with Christ's teachings? Pray for God's guidance in living consistently as His ambassador, seeking opportunities to demonstrate His love and share His truth with others. Commit to living with integrity and gratitude, recognizing every aspect of your life as an opportunity to magnify God's glory.

Prayer:
Dear Lord Jesus, I commit myself to living out the gospel in every aspect of my life. Help me to speak and act in ways that honor You and point others to Your love and truth. Fill me with Your Spirit so that I may reflect Your character and bring glory to Your name. May my life be a testimony of Your grace and a light that draws others to You. In Your precious name, I pray. Amen.

Action Point:
Choose one area of your daily life—whether at home, work, school, or in your community—and intentionally seek to live out Colossians 3:17.

Focus on speaking words of encouragement, showing kindness, and demonstrating integrity in your interactions. Look for opportunities to share the gospel through your actions and attitudes, inviting others to know Christ through your example. Keep a journal to reflect on how God uses your commitment to living out the gospel to impact those around you and contribute to the revival of hearts within your church community.

National Revival (Days 21-30)

Day 21: Righteous Leadership

Bible Passage:
"Righteousness exalts a nation, but sin is a disgrace to any people." – Proverbs 14:34 (NASB)

Thought for the Day:
Proverbs 14:34 reminds us of the profound impact of righteous leadership on a nation. Righteousness—living in alignment with God's standards of justice, integrity, and moral principles—uplifts and brings blessing to a nation. Conversely, sin and moral decay lead to condemnation and spiritual decline. As citizens, our responsibility includes praying for and supporting leaders who govern with righteousness and uphold biblical values. National revival begins with righteous leadership that seeks God's wisdom, acknowledges His sovereignty, and governs with integrity and compassion. When leaders prioritize righteousness, they set a foundation for God's blessing and spiritual renewal to flourish throughout the land.

Today, reflect on the state of leadership in your nation. Are your leaders guided by principles of righteousness and justice? Pray for God's wisdom and discernment to be upon national leaders, so that they may govern with integrity and seek His guidance in decision-making. Commit to actively engaging in civic responsibilities, including voting and advocating for policies that uphold biblical values and promote the common good.

Prayer:
Heavenly Father, I lift up the leaders of my nation to You. Grant them wisdom and courage to govern with righteousness and justice. May they seek Your will in all decisions and lead our nation according to Your Word. Strengthen those who stand for truth and righteousness. Guide us as citizens to support and pray for our leaders for the spiritual revival and blessing of our nation. In Jesus' name, I pray. Amen.

Action Point:
Educate yourself on the values and policies of political candidates and elected officials in your nation. Pray for discernment to vote wisely and responsibly in elections, choosing leaders who prioritize righteousness and uphold biblical principles. Engage in respectful dialogue with others about the importance of righteous leadership and encourage fellow believers to participate actively in civic engagement. Support initiatives and organizations that promote biblical values and contribute to the spiritual and moral renewal of our nation.

Day 22: Praying for Authorities

Bible Passage:
"First of all, then, I urge that requests, prayers, intercession, and thanksgiving be made in behalf of all people, for kings and all who are in authority, so that we may lead a tranquil and quiet life in all godliness and dignity." – 1 Timothy 2:1-2 (NASB)

Thought for the Day:
In 1 Timothy 2:1-2, Paul exhorts believers to pray for all people, especially for those in positions of authority. This includes national leaders, governmental officials, and those who shape policies and laws. Prayer for authorities is essential for promoting peace, justice, and the ability to live out our faith freely. As Christians, our prayers have the power to influence decisions and policies that impact our nation's spiritual and moral landscape. When we intercede for our leaders, we align ourselves with God's desire for His will to be done on

earth as it is in Heaven, fostering an environment where righteousness can flourish and national revival can take root.

Today, commit to praying earnestly for the leaders of your nation. Ask God to grant them wisdom, integrity, and a heart that seeks His guidance in their decisions. Pray for protection from corruption and for policies that uphold biblical values of justice, compassion, and moral integrity. As you lift up prayers for authorities, trust in God's sovereignty and His ability to work through leaders to bring about His purposes and blessings for your nation.

Prayer:
Heavenly Father, I lift up to You the leaders of my nation. Grant them wisdom to govern justly and with integrity. May they seek Your guidance and lead our country in ways that honor You and promote righteousness. Protect them from temptation and corruption. Use their decisions to bring peace and prosperity, allowing us to live quiet lives in godliness and holiness. In Jesus' name, I pray. Amen.

Action Point:
Create a list of government leaders—from local to national levels—and commit to praying specifically for them each day. Use 1 Timothy 2:1-2 as a guide, praying for wisdom, integrity, and a heart receptive to God's leading in their decision-making. Consider joining or initiating a prayer group focused on interceding for authorities and governmental leaders, fostering a community dedicated to seeking God's guidance and blessing upon your nation through prayer.

Day 23: Justice and Mercy

Bible Passage:
"He has told you, mortal one, what is good; and what does the Lord require of you but to do justice, to love kindness, and to walk humbly with your God?" – Micah 6:8 (NASB)

Thought for the Day:
Micah 6:8 outlines God's expectations for His people: to act justly, love kindness, and walk humbly with Him. As we consider America's need for revival, these principles are foundational. Acting justly involves upholding righteousness and fairness in our dealings with others and advocating for justice in our society. Loving mercy compels us to extend compassion, forgiveness, and grace to those in need, reflecting God's heart for reconciliation and restoration. Walking humbly with God requires a posture of surrender, seeking His guidance, and aligning our lives with His will. A national revival begins when individuals and communities embrace these principles, leading to transformed hearts, relationships, and societal structures.

Today, reflect on how you can actively pursue justice and mercy in your community and nation. Pray for discernment to recognize opportunities to advocate for justice and extend mercy to others. Ask God to empower you to live in alignment with His will, humbly seeking His guidance and reflecting His character in all your actions and interactions.

Prayer:
Heavenly Father, You are just and merciful. Help me to act justly in my interactions with others and to love kindness as You do. Guide me in walking humbly with You, seeking Your will, and following Your ways. May my life reflect Your righteousness and compassion, contributing to the revival of justice and mercy in my nation. In Jesus' name, I pray. Amen.

Action Point:
Identify a social justice issue or area of need in your community or nation. Take practical steps to advocate for justice and extend kindness in this area. This could involve volunteering with organizations that promote justice, supporting initiatives that provide kindness to the marginalized, or advocating for policy changes that reflect biblical principles of justice and kindness. Commit to being a voice for righteousness and compassion, actively working towards societal transformation and revival in your sphere of influence.

Day 24: Healing the Land

Bible Passage:

"[If] My people who are called by My name humble themselves, and pray and seek My face, and turn from their wicked ways, then I will hear from Heaven, and I will forgive their sin and will heal their land."
– 2 Chronicles 7:14 (NASB)

Thought for the Day:

In 2 Chronicles 7:14, God outlines a clear path to healing and revival for a nation. He calls His people to humble themselves, pray, seek His face, and turn from sinful ways. This verse reveals God's desire for spiritual renewal and restoration at a national level, emphasizing the importance of repentance, prayer, and obedience to His Word. Healing the land begins in the hearts of God's people—their humility, prayerfulness, and commitment to living in alignment with His will. As believers, our responsibility is to lead the way in seeking God's forgiveness and transformative power for our nation, trusting in His promise to hear our prayers and bring healing.

Today, consider the spiritual condition of your nation and your role in its revival. Are there areas where you need to humble yourself before God? Are you fervently praying for God's healing and restoration in your land? Reflect on how you can actively participate in the process of national revival by aligning your life with God's principles and interceding for your nation's spiritual awakening.

Prayer:

Heavenly Father, I humble myself before You and seek Your face. Forgive us, as a nation, for our sins and shortcomings. Heal our land, O Lord, and bring spiritual revival to our people. Help us to turn from our wicked ways and to embrace Your truth and righteousness. May Your Holy Spirit move mightily across our nation, drawing many to repentance and faith in Jesus Christ. In Jesus' name, I pray. Amen.

Action Point:
Commit to praying daily for national revival, specifically following the pattern laid out in 2 Chronicles 7:14. Dedicate time each day to pray for humility among God's people, repentance for national sins, a renewed hunger for God's Word, and a turning away from sinful practices in society. Engage in corporate prayer gatherings or initiatives focused on seeking God's healing and revival for your nation. Additionally, consider fasting as a way to intensify your prayers and seek God's face more earnestly for national transformation.

Day 25: Christian Influence in Society

Bible Passage:
"You are the salt of the earth; but if the salt has become tasteless, how can it be made salty again? It is no longer good for anything, except to be thrown out and trampled underfoot by people. You are the light of the world. A city set on a hill cannot be hidden; nor do people light a lamp and put it under a basket, but on the lampstand, and it gives light to all who are in the house. Your light must shine before people in such a way that they may see your good works, and glorify your Father who is in Heaven." – Matthew 5:13-16 (NIV)

Thought for the Day:
Matthew 5:13-16 teaches us about the transformative influence Christians are meant to have in society. As salt preserves and enhances flavor and light dispels darkness, so are believers called to impact their surroundings positively. Our lives should reflect the values of God's Kingdom—such as love, justice, mercy, and truth—so that others may witness our good deeds and glorify God. In a nation seeking revival, Christians play a crucial role as ambassadors of Christ, bringing His light into every sphere of society, from politics to education, from business to the arts. When we live out our faith boldly and authentically, we contribute to the moral and spiritual renewal of our nation.

Today, reflect on how you are influencing your community and society as a Christian. Are you actively living out your faith in ways that reflect

Christ's character? Pray for God's guidance to be a faithful witness and light-bearer in your sphere of influence, impacting others for His Kingdom. Seek opportunities to demonstrate God's love through acts of kindness, justice, and compassion, thereby shining brightly in a world that desperately needs His light.

Prayer:
Heavenly Father, thank You for calling me to be the salt and light in this world. Help me to live a life that reflects Your love, truth, and grace. Empower me by Your Spirit to influence my community and nation for Your glory. May my actions and words point others to You, that they may come to know Your saving grace and experience Your revival. Use me, Lord, to make a difference in my sphere of influence. In Jesus' name, I pray. Amen.

Action Point:
Identify one area of influence in your community or workplace where you can intentionally demonstrate Christ's love and values. Whether through volunteering, advocating for justice, or engaging in respectful dialogue about faith, commit to being a positive influence for Christ. Consider joining or supporting organizations that promote biblical principles in societal issues. Pray for opportunities to share your faith and for God's guidance in effectively shining His light in your community, contributing to America's national revival through your actions and witness.

Day 26: Revival in the Marketplace

Bible Passage:
"Whatever you do, do your work heartily, as for the Lord and not for people, knowing that it is from the Lord that you will receive the reward of the inheritance. It is the Lord Christ whom you serve." – Colossians 3:23-24 (NASB)

Thought for the Day:
Colossians 3:23-24 emphasizes the significance of our work as unto the Lord. In the context of America's national revival, the marketplace—where we spend a significant portion of our lives—is a critical sphere for God's influence and transformation. As Christians, our jobs and businesses are opportunities to glorify God through our diligence, integrity, and service to others. When we work with excellence and integrity, treating colleagues, customers, and competitors with respect and fairness, we reflect God's character and contribute to the moral and spiritual fabric of society. Revival in the marketplace begins with Christians embracing their roles as ambassadors of Christ, impacting workplaces with His love and truth.

Today, consider how you can bring revival to your workplace or business. Are you working with diligence and integrity, as if serving the Lord Himself? Pray for God's wisdom and strength to excel in your work, honoring Him in all you do. Seek opportunities to demonstrate Christ's love through your interactions and decisions. Whether through mentoring colleagues, advocating for ethical practices, or sharing your faith with integrity, commit to being a catalyst for revival in the marketplace.

Prayer:
Heavenly Father, I commit my work to You today. Help me to work diligently and with integrity. May my actions and attitudes in the workplace reflect Your love and truth. Use me as a vessel for Your Kingdom's purposes, impacting my colleagues and customers for Your glory. Grant me opportunities to share Your gospel and to be a witness for Your revival in the marketplace. In Jesus' name, I pray. Amen.

Action Point:
Reflect on your work or business practices. Identify one area where you can improve or bring more of God's Kingdom's values into your daily work routine. It could be through showing more kindness to coworkers, going above and beyond in service to clients, or being more intentional about integrating your faith into your professional life. Seek God's guidance and take practical steps to implement these

changes, trusting Him to use your efforts to bring about His revival in the marketplace.

Day 27: Unity Among Believers

Bible Passage:
"I am not asking on behalf of these alone, but also for those who believe in Me through their word, that they may all be one; just as You, Father, are in Me and I in You, that they also may be in Us, so that the world may believe that You sent Me." – John 17:20-21 (NASB)

Thought for the Day:
In John 17, Jesus prays for unity among believers—a unity that reflects the intimate relationship between the Father and the Son. This unity is not just a pleasant idea but a powerful witness to the world of God's love and the truth of Jesus' mission. As we pray for America's national revival, unity among Christians is crucial. When we are united in purpose, spirit, and love, we demonstrate the reality of Christ's message and draw others to faith. Unity doesn't mean uniformity but a shared commitment to Jesus Christ and His gospel, transcending differences for the sake of His Kingdom.

Today, reflect on the unity of believers in your community and nation. Are there divisions or barriers that hinder collaboration and mutual support among Christians? Pray for God's Spirit to bring reconciliation, healing, and unity among believers, so that we may truly reflect Christ's love to the world. Commit to fostering unity by seeking opportunities to collaborate with other believers, supporting ministries and initiatives that promote unity, and praying earnestly for the unity of the Church in America.

Prayer:
Heavenly Father, I thank You for the gift of unity among believers. Help us, Lord, to be united in spirit and purpose, just as Jesus prayed. Remove any barriers that divide us and hinder Your Kingdom's work. May our unity be a testimony to the world of Your love and truth.

Strengthen our bonds of fellowship and empower us to work together for Your glory and the advancement of Your Kingdom. In Jesus' name, I pray. Amen.

Action Point:
Reach out to a fellow believer or Christian organization with whom you haven't interacted much before. Initiate a conversation or collaboration that fosters unity and cooperation in advancing God's Kingdom's purposes. Attend a joint prayer gathering or event hosted by different churches or denominations in your area, actively participating in efforts to pray for national revival and unity among believers. Support initiatives that promote unity and reconciliation within the Church, demonstrating Christ's love and unity to a divided world.

Day 28: Spiritual Awakening

Bible Passage:
"Arise, shine; for your light has come, and the glory of the Lord has risen upon you. For behold, darkness will cover the earth and deep darkness the peoples; but the Lord will rise upon you and His glory will appear upon you." – Isaiah 60:1-2 (NASB)

Thought for the Day:
Isaiah 60:1-2 speaks of a call to spiritual awakening—a moment when God's light breaks through the darkness that covers the earth. In times of national turmoil and moral decline, God calls His people to arise and shine, for His glory is upon them. Spiritual awakening begins with a renewed awareness of God's presence and power. It involves turning away from darkness and embracing the light of His truth and righteousness. As believers, we are called to be beacons of hope and truth in our communities and nation, reflecting God's glory and leading others to experience His saving grace.

Today, reflect on the spiritual condition of America and your role in its revival. Are you actively seeking God's presence and guidance in your life? Pray for a personal spiritual awakening and for God to pour out

His Spirit across your nation. Ask Him to use you as an instrument of His light and truth in your sphere of influence. Commit to living a life that shines brightly for Christ, demonstrating His love and proclaiming His gospel to those around you.

Prayer:
Heavenly Father, I thank You for Your promise of light and glory in the midst of darkness. Awaken my spirit, O Lord, and fill me with Your presence and power. Shine Your light through me, that others may see Your glory and come to know You. Use me as Your instrument of revival in my community and nation. May Your Spirit move mightily, drawing many hearts to repentance and faith in Jesus Christ. In His name, I pray. Amen.

Action Point:
Commit to spending dedicated time in prayer and personal worship each day, seeking God's presence and guidance for personal and national revival. Consider fasting as a way to deepen your spiritual sensitivity and dependence on God during this time of seeking spiritual awakening. Share your faith boldly and lovingly with those around you, pointing them towards the hope found in Christ amidst the darkness of the world. Look for opportunities to participate in or initiate prayer gatherings focused on seeking God's spiritual awakening and revival in America.

Day 29: Standing for Truth

Bible Passage:
"Stand firm therefore, having belted your waist with truth, and having put on the breastplate of righteousness." – Ephesians 6:14 (NASB)

Thought for the Day:
Ephesians 6:14 exhorts believers to stand firm with the belt of truth buckled around their waist. In the midst of cultural shifts and moral relativism, standing for truth is crucial for America's national revival. The truth we stand for is not merely a set of beliefs but the very essence

of God's Word and His character. As Christians, we are called to uphold God's truth with unwavering conviction and courage, regardless of societal pressures or opposition. Standing for truth means aligning our lives with God's moral standards and boldly proclaiming His truth in a world that desperately needs His light.

Today, reflect on how you are standing for truth in your personal life and within your sphere of influence. Are there areas where compromise or silence has crept in? Pray for God's strength and wisdom to uphold His truth faithfully. Ask Him to embolden you to speak truth in love, defend biblical principles, and live out His truth in your actions and words. Commit to being a beacon of truth in your community, demonstrating Christ's righteousness and love through your unwavering commitment to His Word.

Prayer:
Heavenly Father, I thank You for Your truth revealed in Your Word. Grant me the courage and wisdom to stand firm in Your truth, even when faced with opposition or cultural pressure. Help me to live a life that honors You, upholding Your standards of righteousness and love. Use me, Lord, to be a voice for Your truth in my community and nation. May Your truth prevail and bring about spiritual awakening and revival in America. In Jesus' name, I pray. Amen.

Action Point:
Identify one specific area where truth is being challenged or compromised in your community or nation. Take a proactive step to advocate for biblical truth in that area—whether through writing a letter, participating in a respectful dialogue, or engaging in advocacy efforts. Seek opportunities to share biblical truths with others, showing the relevance and transformative power of God's Word in everyday life. Pray for discernment and boldness to stand for truth in all circumstances, trusting God to use your efforts for His glory and America's national revival.

Day 30: Hope for the Future

Bible Passage:
"'For I know the plans that I have for you,' declares the Lord, 'plans for prosperity and not for disaster, to give you a future and a hope.'" – Jeremiah 29:11 (NASB)

Thought for the Day:
Jeremiah 29:11 is a powerful reminder of God's sovereign plans and purposes for His people. In the context of America's national revival, this verse offers hope and assurance that God's intentions for His people are good. Even amidst challenges, uncertainties, and moral crises, God promises a future filled with hope and prosperity for those who seek Him. As we pray for revival in our nation, we can trust that God has a divine plan to bring about spiritual renewal and restoration. Our hope is not in human efforts alone but in the steadfast promises of God, who faithfully fulfills His promises in His time and way.

Today, reflect on God's promises for your life and for America. Are you trusting in His plans and His timing? Pray for renewed hope and faith in God's sovereign control over national affairs. Ask Him to strengthen your faith and fill you with His peace as you await His perfect timing for revival. Commit to being a vessel of hope and encouragement in your community, sharing the gospel message of hope and pointing others towards God's promises.

Prayer:
Heavenly Father, thank You for Your promise of hope and a future through Jesus Christ. I surrender my fears and uncertainties to You, trusting in Your perfect plans for my life and for our nation. Renew my hope, O Lord, and strengthen my faith in Your sovereign control. May Your will be done on earth as it is in Heaven. Use me, Lord, to share Your hope with others and to be a light of encouragement in our world. In Jesus' name, I pray. Amen.

Action Point:
Write down Jeremiah 29:11 and place it somewhere prominent where you will see it daily—a reminder of God's promises and His faithfulness. Take time to pray specifically for America's national revival, asking God to work in the hearts of leaders, influencers, and citizens across the nation. Look for opportunities to share messages of hope and encouragement with those around you, pointing them toward the eternal hope found in Christ. Trust in God's timing for revival, continuing to pray fervently and faithfully for His Kingdom to come and His will to be done in America.

Day 31: A Call to Continue

Bible Passage:
"Brothers and sisters, I do not regard myself as having taken hold of it yet; but one thing I do: forgetting what lies behind and reaching forward to what lies ahead, I press on toward the goal for the prize of the upward call of God in Christ Jesus." – Philippians 3:13-14 (NASB)

Thought for the Day:
Philippians 3:13-14 encapsulates the Christian journey as a continuous pursuit of spiritual growth and obedience to God's calling. As we conclude this devotional series on revival, let us heed Paul's exhortation to press on in our faith and service to God. Revival is not a one-time event but an ongoing process of personal and communal renewal in Christ. It requires a commitment to seek God wholeheartedly, repent of sin, live in obedience to His Word, and share the gospel boldly with others. As we look ahead, let us fix our eyes on Jesus, the author and perfecter of our faith, and continue to pursue His Kingdom's purposes with zeal and perseverance.

Today, reflect on the journey of revival you've embarked upon through this devotional series. How has God spoken to you? How have you grown spiritually? Give thanks for His faithfulness and grace in your life. Pray for a renewed passion and commitment to live out the principles of revival daily. Ask God to empower you by His Spirit to continue seeking Him fervently and to be a catalyst for revival in your family, church, community, and nation.

Prayer:
Heavenly Father, thank You for the journey of revival You have led us on through Your Word. As we conclude this devotional series, I commit myself anew to You and Your Kingdom's purposes. Help me, Lord, to forget what is behind and to press on toward the goal of knowing You more deeply and making You known. Grant me Your strength and wisdom to live a life worthy of Your calling, sharing Your love and truth with those around me. May revival continue to spread in my heart, my community, and across our nation. In Jesus' name, I pray. Amen.

Action Point:
Commit to a daily habit of prayer, Bible study, and reflection on God's Word beyond this devotional series. Set specific spiritual goals for growth in your faith and obedience to God's Word. Consider joining or starting a small group focused on prayer and revival, where members can support and encourage one another in their spiritual journeys. Look for opportunities to serve and share the gospel in your community, actively participating in God's mission to bring revival to hearts and lives around you.

About the Author

Over the last forty years, Chris Widener has spent significant time across three professions: pastoral ministry, public speaking, and politics. As a pastor, he started and oversaw the founding of three churches in the greater Seattle area. In speaking, he became one of the most well-known public speakers in America and has been named one of the top 100 leadership speakers by Inc. Magazine and one of the top 10 sales speakers by Success Magazine. He is also a member of the Motivational Speakers Hall of Fame. In politics, he has served as a speech coach to many political figures running for Governor, Senator, Congress, and the Presidency. One thing Chris has seen after being involved in these three endeavors at the highest levels is that the only answer for America is God. Not self-help. Not any politician.

Only God can save America.

Chris' desire is for *The Coming American Revival* to be a catalyst for American Christians to take seriously the call for revival and to seek God for a move of the Holy Spirit across America.

Chris and his wife Denise live in Chattanooga, TN.

To have Chris speak at your church, business, or organization, you can email him at Chris@ChrisWidener.com or call 877-212-4747. You can visit him on the web at http://ChrisWidener.com, where you can find his dozens of other books and audio programs.

For bulk orders of this book, please call 877–212-4747.

Enjoy more books by Chris Widener

Four Seasons
Are you prepared for the inevitable?

Praying Through the Proverbs
Timeless wisdom, profound insights

Lasting Impact
You were designed to make an impact

**How to Talk to Anybody,
Anywhere, Anytime**
3-Steps to prepare for any
social situation

Learn More Here

Discover How People Respond to God's Gospel Message

God has a perfect plan for your life to experience his radical love.

Learn More Here

Made in the USA
Columbia, SC
20 October 2024

44333185R00102